Unlocking the Body's Wisdom

Accessing Your Healing Power from Within

Shara Ogin

Copyright, 2021, by Shara Ogin—all rights reserved.

No portion of this book may be reproduced or transmitted in any form, electronic or mechanical, photocopying or otherwise, without the written permission of the publisher and by the United States copyright laws.

Limit of Liability/Disclaimer of Warranty: The information presented here is designed to help you to live a happier, healthier life, and by no means is meant to be a substitute for any treatment or protocol anyone from the medical establishment has prescribed or recommended.

The advice and strategies contained herein may not be suitable for everyone.

The application of protocols and information in this book is the choice of each reader, who needs to assume full responsibility for his or her understanding, interpretations, and results. The author/publisher assumes no responsibility for the outcomes, actions, or choices of any reader.

While all of the case histories and stories are true, some of the names and identifying details have been changed in this book to protect the privacy of individuals.

Edited by Laurel Ornitz
Cover designed by Tahir Tariq

Dedication

This book is dedicated to all of the wonderful teachers I have had over the years who have taught me how to heal my own internal wounds and connect intimately with my physical body, my heart, and my third eye. I give thanks to all of those who believed in me along this journey and helped me to bring my gifts out into the world to help others.

And to my greatest gift of all, my beautiful young daughter—she is the living proof of how all my years of inner work and personal growth have paid off.

Content

Introduction .... *i*

Part I: Back to Balance **1**

    Chapter 1: Our Balancing Systems 3

    Chapter 2: The Analyzer, the Heart, and the Third Eye 9

    Chapter 3: Entering the World of the Pain-Body 19

Part II: Family Systems **27**

    Chapter 4: Our Longing to Belong 29

    Chapter 5: Guilt and Sin, Good and Bad 43

Part III: Physiology, Beliefs, and Emotions **49**

    Chapter 6: Effects of Negative Thinking 51

    Chapter 7: Muscular States of Emotions 55

    Chapter 8: Thoughts and Beliefs 61

Part IV: Diagnoses, Root Causes, and Perspectives for Healing **69**

    Chapter 9: Healing From the Root 71

    Chapter 10: Diagnoses Present Themselves as Themes 75

Part V: Potentiating Your Life 79

Chapter 11: Your Soul's Journey 81

Chapter 12: A Journey in Search of Our Life's Purpose 85

Chapter 13: Lifting the Veil 89

Healing from the Root (Instructions) 94

Diagnoses/Ailments Chart 95
Other Useful Healing Tools and Techniques 178

Unleash Your Purpose Workbook (Free Link) 183

About the Author 187

References 189

Introduction

What if I told you that you had the power to heal your body just by changing your thoughts, beliefs, and behaviors?

I know, this sounds too good to be true. Trust me, I was just as skeptical when I picked up Louis Hay's book, You Can Heal your Life, in 2007 suggesting that the root cause of illness was related to our thoughts. Prior to this time, I had always thought energy healing and thinking yourself well was snake oil and not to be trusted.

After-all,I had been working in mainstream medicine as an Occupational therapist (for 25 years) and an Ergonomist (for 3 years), and never once doubted the reasons why my patient's had the diagnoses they had, nor the standardized treatment protocols for them.

Never prior to this time did I believe the client had the power to truly heal themselves without medical intervention, nor did I see a correlation between my clients' unhappy marriages, anger, and depression (which they frequently confided in me), and their diagnoses or illness. After all, I come from a family of scientific thinkers. With my father and 80% of the men in my family being traditional physicians, I was sculpted to believe in evidence-based medicine.

My background comes from mainstream science. In fact, I never believed in psychics or put much thought into metaphysics. For myself, just like all the other Ogin's in my family, our bodies would cringe every time we heard the word "psychic" or "energy healer." I still to this day have great respect for the medical model and incorporate it for my own personal health and wellness.

However, I went through a deep profound shift or what some may call a "spiritual awakening" between the years 2013-2014. Prior to this time, my life consisted of working 9 a.m.-5 p.m. as and Occupational Therapist, coming home, working out, making dinner, and going to bed feeling incredibly lonely, lost and unfulfilled. This enormous sense of dissatisfaction became the catalyst that propelled me to enter into a clairvoyant school in the year 2011 and delve deep into my psyche.

Although I only initially committed to a 7-week meditation class at this school (Psychic Horizons in San Francisco), I ended up studying there four days a week for the next four years. I simply wanted to learn how to be happy and satisfied with the life I was living, and I desperately wanted to fall in love.

Yet the story of what really lead me on my spiritual journey stems back to my teenage years. When I was 16-19 years old, I struggled with anorexia, exacerbated by years of social anxieties and feelings of rejection and being on the outside of social groups.

The pain from this experience never really abated. Rather, it was temporarily suppressed for a few years, and then resurfaced again when I was around the age of 22-25. This time it presented itself differently where my body image was intact, yet I had severe digestive issues. Nothing I consumed was breaking down properly.

I remember one morning I ate two hard boiled eggs, and by that evening I was burping up what smelled and tasted like rotten eggs. My throat glands were often swollen from belching up so often, I had brain fog for most of the day and my entire body felt extremely lethargic. Due to the discomfort eating caused me, I found it easier to refrain from eating altogether, especially when I knew I would be interacting with other people.

I hated the way I looked, I hated the way I felt, I hated the person who I was, and all I really wanted to do was hide in my shame and misery.

My father, being an Anesthesiologist, took me to a G.I. Doc, an Internist, and every specialist he could, yet they found nothing.

Finally, I found a naturopathic doctor who after performing several tests said I was lacking every digestive enzyme needed to break down food. He put me on a candida diet amongst other things, yet by that time it was already too late. At 5'7" and weighing a mere 99 pounds, I needed to be hospitalized, and was admitted to an outpatient eating disorder program.

Looking back upon this experience, I now see that what I needed more than anything was to feel my inherit worth and to believe nothing was wrong with me. I needed to learn self-acceptance.

This experience is a large part of what propelled me on a lifelong journey of self-discovery work. A journey towards finding self-love. Not only to find my confidence and belief in myself, but to find my genius, my excellence, and my AWESOMENESS!

I spent one year living at the San Francisco Zen Center studying Buddhism (2000), I participated in transformational workshops regularly since 2002 (such as Arete, the Institute of Self Actualization, and neuro-linguistic programming trainings), I took two years of coaching trainings, completed a four-year Feldenkrais® somatic training, learned reiki and other such modalities, and I lived in intentional communities dedicated to connection and intimacy. I was blessed with some of the most wonderful teachers who helped me to grow and progress. I eventually came to the realization that I no longer needed to hide the parts of myself I considered undesirable and shameful, and finally, by the ripe age of 39, I was finally ready to share all of myself authentically and openly with others.

Yet the icing on the cake came in the year 2015-2016, upon completing my clairvoyant studies. This is the year everything in my life changed. Through this program, I developed the ability to "see" through a clairvoyant's eye which gave me a new perspective on the world.

I healed my residual limiting thoughts and beliefs as well as so many of my traumas and wounds of past. I had succeeded in shifting almost every aspect of my internal landscape to one much more congruent with the truth of who I really am.

I met my husband that year, and two years later, at the age of 47, got married, bore a beautiful daughter, and fulfilled every one of my dreams and desires.

I finally learned how to find that place of inner peace and fulfillment, and shortly after, people started to seek me out…to find their own answers and healing.

I had no idea what the word "clairvoyance" even meant prior to entering Psychic Horizons school. Clairvoyance, also known as extrasensory perception, is the ability to perceive matters beyond the range of ordinary perception.

Now, I can close my eyes, quiet my mind, ask myself a question, and Wala, a representative picture containing the information I need is right there out in front of me (more about this in Section IV). With continual practice, I developed the ability to "see" precisely what was blocking a person from attracting love, making money, or finding a job one is passionate about. Combining my work as a Feldenkrais Practitioner®, energy healer, and occupational therapist, I developed the ability to see what was keeping people in pain and lying at the root of their disease and illness.

I had been working with patients with pain or disease in the medical profession since 1994, yet when I began to work with them from a clairvoyant perspective, I started to notice certain patterns my medically trained eye had been blind to seeing. About 5 years ago, I started to take notes about what I found to be the root cause for each injury and diagnosis, and low and behold, there turned out to be patterns and predictable correlations for each one. And this laid the foundation for this book, which I have dedicated much of the past several years to completing.

I have charted these findings for you in the back of this book. The chart outlines 150+ diagnoses, root causes, and perspectives for healing from a mind/body perspective. My greatest hope is that you will keep this book as a reference manual on your bookshelf, referring to it anytime a friend, a client, a family member, or even yourself has an ache or an illness, and utilize it as sort of an encyclopedia towards wellness.

This book will introduce you to some amazing truths that will change your life regarding your body, your health, and what you are on this planet to do! While these truths in and of themselves may excite you and transform the way you had previously viewed illness, disease, and trauma, you will also learn that absolutely NOTHING is set in stone regarding your health and wellness. There is no predestined path you cannot reprogram or change. You CAN set yourself on course for living a healthier, happier, and more fulfilling life no matter where you come from or what condition you are currently in!

People often find me when the normal channels of medicine or psychology fail them, and I have made it one of my lifelong goals to assist my clients in the relief of their discomfort (emotional and physical that is) and to help them step into a richer, more fulfilling life.

Healing from the inside out will assist you with not only resolving your physical ailments, it will also point you in the trajectory towards what you were put on this planet to be doing! This is not a claim I make lightly, nor it does not come without a fair admonition. The exploration into self is not easy.

The work to restore your body to homeostasis or balance will require a great deal of time, energy, and commitment. It will require you to shine a light in the darkest of corners and it will force you to face your fears and your truths (when you are ready). This journey will require you to quiet your mind, tune inward, and listen to the small quiet voices inside that are vying for your attention.

These parts I speak of are usually formed in early childhood and lie hidden in the protective programming we developed to shield ourselves from what we perceived to be a real physical danger. In other words, we developed physiological responses and behaviors as a means of coping with the world around us (more about this in Part II).

The unfortunate reality is that most of us are still utilizing these same protective mechanisms, even though the actual danger is no longer present. We may over contract our muscles, halt, and pull in our breath and create a subconscious wall of protection around our lungs despite the fact that these physiological reactions are very likely working against us, inhibiting our abilities to move quickly and with ease. (More about this in Part III).

Our bodies are so accustomed to reacting as if the metaphorical saber-tooth tiger is still around when truly such a danger doesn't even exist. It never did! Yet as young children, our brains weren't developed enough to believe otherwise.

You may have for instance, thought that when your parents got divorced or your father left, it meant he didn't love you, or it was you who did something wrong and pushed him away. Yet now it's time to pick up our pens and rewrite our stories of devastation and demise.

In my first book, *A Quick Guide to Easing Pain in the Workplace and Beyond*, I referenced the fact that most people are overusing the distal parts of themselves (such as the fingers and wrists) more than is necessary for the task at hand, while the more proximal parts are being underutilized (such as the pelvis and thighs). This factor alone can eventually lead to pain, not to mention exhaustion, lack of balance, and fatigue.

All our movement and contraction patterns throughout our body are in reality a culmination of our life story. Every time our mother yelled at us, or when we were picked on at school, or when we felt less important than our older siblings sitting at the dinner table, our bodies responded in subtle ways.

The more frequent or traumatic these experiences were, the deeper the neural imprint. All this information is housed deep in our unconscious and forms the basis of how we move, think, and act in the world today.

Every fear, trauma, struggle, or unmet need has been encoded into our DNA and influences the way we look, feel and act to this day. Simply observing the way a person holds their head, clenches their muscles, and walks through the world can provide a great deal of information about who the person is. Their triumphs, strengths, hardships, and aspirations of grandeur; it's all right there.

Do they have a heavy down step of their flat right foot, representative of the heaviness and hardships of life, or do they walk across the room with a light pounce? If nothing else, one can see it deep in the pearls of another's eyes or in the harbors of their face. Are the sides of their lips turned upwards from an abundance of smiling or is there a furrow between their eyebrows from life's struggles. (More about this in Part III).

Honing your skills of observation and noticing, especially within yourself is a great first step! The next step is to release our stuck emotions, meet the unmet needs we experienced as children, and reprogram our entire system with a new way of thinking, feeling, and acting. Easy Peasy, right?

That's a joke. Yet the good news is this entire book + workbook will take you on a journey to do just that. And when we do, we might begin to notice synchronicities and magic all around us.

Also, throughout this book, I made numerous references to my other books, videos, and free resources which I believe can assist your healing journey. I will list these resources at the back of the book.

You CAN fully excel no matter where you come from, how old you are, or how badly you have been bullied and bruised. This book (and the accompanying workbook) will guide you through various processes to help you to access YOUR Healing Powers from Within!

How to Use This Book

This book is divided into five parts.

The first part will be a thorough guide to learning to listen to our inner truths and messages of our higher self, our heart, and our third eye.

The second part dives deep into family and ancestral patterns and their mysterious impact on our current life.

The third part examines the interconnection between our emotions, physiological states of the body, thoughts, and beliefs.

The fourth part provides a quick reference guide to understanding the root of specific ailments and disease states from a holistic metaphysical perspective. It also offers simple healing suggestions (mostly focused in the realm of our thoughts, beliefs, and behaviors).

The fifth part unravels the deeper meaning of our pain states from the perspective of the soul. This part opens the doors to better understanding YOUR chosen destiny.

~~~

Pain can be viewed from many different angles. First, there is physical. This includes the way we hold ourselves and tense our muscles from everything from the way we pull our right shoulders up toward our ears and pound the keys of our keyboard when we type to inhibiting our breath at work.

Secondly, there are the emotional and psychosocial dimensions of pain, which much of this book will focus upon. This includes feeling work deadlines and pressures, feeling like we are inept, unlovable, or not good enough, or feeling isolated and alone in our predicament and experiences.

And thirdly, we can categorize things that occur beyond what we can see, feel, or hear, that which occurs beyond our fourth-dimensional reality.

This includes ancestral and karmic patterns, as well as our connection with Source. Much of this will be addressed in this book.

Throughout this book, there are numerous meditations and exercises. There is also an accompanying workbook I have created that is filled with exercises and strategies too in-depth to actually fit into this book. If you are a coach, psychotherapist, or someone who helps others with emotional or physical pain, or if you yourself have pain or are simply on a quest for self-discovery and meaning, I highly recommend this workbook for you as an accompaniment to this book.

I also made a lot of references to a somatic healing technique I absolutely love and integrate quite a bit into my work called Feldenkrais. Feldenkrais helps with the re-education of our bones, muscles, and the entire nervous system, rewiring the way they interact with one another toward their optimal state. The written and verbal processes and exercises in this book will help with mental rewiring and the somatic Feldenkrais lessons will help with physical rewiring.

I believe true healing involves a combination of both the body and the mind (and the spirit, which will be addressed later in this book). Although there are only a few mini-Feldenkrais lessons written into this book, I have plenty of references and resources for audio and video lessons. I will list these as well as my other resources which I believe can assist your healing journey at the back of the book.

All the exercises in this book are designed as step-by-step instructions to help reveal the roots of your emotional and physical pain, reprogram unhealthy patterns, and heal emotional wounds so you can step into a life that expresses the fullness of who you are.

Who and What is Feldenkrais?

The Feldenkrais method was devised by Moshé Feldenkrais (1904–1984), a Ukrainian-born physicist and mechanical and electrical engineer, who developed the method while rehabilitating from a recurring knee injury, aggravated by years spent practicing judo and playing soccer.

The method can be performed in one of two ways: through a class led by an instructor. known as "Awareness through Movement®," or "ATM®," or through a "hands-on" session where the practitioner provides skilled and directed touch called "Functional Integration®," or "FI®."

The goal of both methods is to decrease the amount of "wasted" energy or effort required for each movement and instead to instill a feeling of fluidity and ease. For ATM lessons, you want to lie on a mat or rug, and the instructor will guide you through small, gentle movement sequences. FI lessons are typically performed on a massage-like table. Allow yourself to sink into a state of noticing and deep relaxation for both. As you do so, more options and opportunities for movement will become available.

During Feldenkrais sessions, there is a strong possibility of "letting go" of deeply embedded muscular holding patterns. People with chronic pain become so habituated to over-contracting their muscles (for instance, in their toes, their jaw, their diaphragm, etc.), when much less muscular effort is actually required for the task at hand, be it getting out of bed, getting dressed, or even just having a conversation. We all do this, in fact. We're all victims of habit, over-utilizing certain parts of ourselves and under-using others in less-than-optimal ways.

Part I

Back to Balance

I have found there is no better tool to help guide us back to balance than through the body. The body holds an infinite storehouse of wisdom. It can help us with everything, from life's daily choices, to how to have more vitality, joy, and fulfillment.

However, most of us have only limited access to such body wisdom. We have rather fallen akin to our daily lives and routines, incorporating the thought patterns, beliefs, and actions deeply influenced by those around us. We have dulled our senses to the chagrin of life, as we know it.

The body is our majestic temple that provides pertinent information as to when an aspect of our mind, body, or spirit is out of alignment.

Chapter 1:

Our Balancing Systems

I want to share with you a secret. It's a secret about finding your blissful calling and life's purpose. Something we all want, right?

It's right there. Hidden deep in the layers of our subconscious and revealed somatically through the body. I have, after all my years of practice, discovered a way to find it.

For practical purposes, a good place to start is to first discover what it is that we don't want, what our bodies are rejecting, and what is throwing off our "balancing systems".

Perhaps we feel pain in our back when working long hours at the job we merely tolerate. Or we experience a clenching at the back of our throat when there's something that wants to be spoken but isn't.

Stuck emotions and unmet needs will eventually peter out into the physical. And when discomfort arises on the physical plane, this often becomes the beacon call to action, redirecting us toward the parts of ourselves most in need of attention.

When we learn to truly listen inwardly, we will encounter aspects of our being that are calling for our attention. These may include parts of ourselves that we want to hide or voids we've been unwilling to acknowledge. Often, they lay hidden from our earliest years and we've developed compensatory habits to prevent us from experiencing the discomfort. Meanwhile, they are throwing off our homeostatic regulating centers, throwing off our alignment and balance.

This book will take you on a journey into the subconscious to heal such imbalances from the origins of where they first occurred up to the now. As this occurs, you will begin to understand how these imbalances actually may serve as an encrypted roadmap toward your destiny. And only YOU have the ability to unlock the encryption code!

Along this journey, I encourage you to keep a beginner's mind and avid curiosity. With a mindset such as this, you are more than likely to gain relevant insights as to what is blocking your highest potential and what action steps will help you to get there.

I am here as a guide to support you along the way.

So, let's begin our deep dive into "the self."

Learning to Listen

The first step toward guiding your body back to balance is simply learning to listen. Though you are listening to your body to a degree now, chances are your body has been talking to you for a while.

You may think that the kink in your neck is from sitting hunched over the computer all day or your back pain is from your poor posture, or it is due to that diagnosis given to you by the doctor. Although this may all be true, when we begin to listen to the wisdom of the body, we discover other pertinent information that may wish to be revealed.

Learning to turn your attention toward your inner wisdom before pain and symptoms set in is a craft. It takes diligent time, practice, and attention. For lack of this, it's no wonder that the experience of tingling, burning, and/or numbness of our fingers are symptoms that are becoming more and more prevalent in the workplace. If you are experiencing these symptoms, it's most likely your nervous system blaring its horn for your attention.

When we're in pain, it is the protocol to see a doctor who will decipher the cause, prescribe medication, and devise the appropriate surgical or treatment plan for you. Occupational and physical therapy is an excellent approach to pain management and post-procedural therapy. Through such therapies, we can receive education on the cause of our pain and how to prevent it, learn body mechanics, stretching, and exercise programs, as well as receive pain-relieving modalities such as electrical stimulation, ultrasound, and heat and cold.

Some of these modalities are extremely effective in healing soft tissue structures, removing excess waste deposits, and helping to block the brain's perception of the pain itself. There is also an uncountable number of manual techniques such as joint mobilizations, massage, Feldenkrais, and cranial sacral therapy that can all be very effective.

I make no attempts to meddle with the knowledge and expertise of the medical profession; instead, my purpose is to enable you to develop the skills to access your own internal body wisdom and to be able to access the truth that lies beneath, in the realm physicians are unable to see, hear, and touch.

I'm curious if you have ever had some sort of medical experience for which your doctors were unable to provide you the answers you needed? Or if the treatment protocol they recommended was more invasive than you were willing?

If so, while going through that experience, did you receive any intuitive hits or insights about something that you may have needed to shift, something that was taking you away from a state of harmony? Even if you did get such an insight, most of us will doubt or even question the relevance to our current pain state.

And then perhaps you got the diagnosis, phew, you're now off the line. They found the cause. "See it's my carpal tunnel or my herniated disc, and so forth, that is at fault!" It's commonplace to think that at this point that you can sit back and see what the doctors and therapists prescribe for you next!

Yet to what degree does the feeling of isolation and rejection from our family or peer groups or the deafness to our soul's calling affect the state of our health? When we struggle to fulfill our destiny and our divine right to live a rich extraordinary life, full of love and purpose, we begin our fatal march toward pain and illness.

As we learn to listen to internal guidance signals, important insights guiding us to a happier, healthier life may be revealed. One of the first steps toward gaining access to answers from within is simply learning to quiet the mind and listen. The basic process for this is as follows:

Basic Steps to Quiet the Mind and Listen

Find a comfortable place where you feel safe, seated either in a chair, with low-back support, seated on the floor on a cushion, or lying down.

Close your eyes. Notice where your attention and focus are, and where you are right now.

Clear your mind—imagine writing all your thoughts onto an imaginary chalkboard out in front of you. Get them all out. Then imagine erasing the chalkboard, clearing away all the thoughts you wrote down. You are welcome to pick your thoughts right back up after this meditation is complete, yet for now, let's move them out of your space. Create a space of emptiness and calm.

Take a few deep nourishing breaths. Full inhale for the count of 4...pause...full exhale for the count of 6.... pause. Continue this four-part circular breathing technique three-to-five more times, refilling your lungs to full capacity, pause, and then exhaling completely, making sure to release the residual air at the base of your lungs, which is still present in a normal exhale. Feel the inhale softening, loosening, and filling your body; on the exhale, visualize the breath releasing everything that's not supposed to be there. (Pause.)

Let all your muscles go, soften, and release them. Allow your body to sink into the surface beneath you. (Pause.)

Coming from a neutral centered space, bring your attention inside of yourself. Listen...notice...and feel. (Pause.)

If thoughts come up (which they will), simply acknowledge them with the word "thinking" and then move them off to the side, quiet your mind, and come back to yourself.

As an option, you can follow the rhythmic flow of your breath coming in and out, in and out. This helps to focus and still the mind.

Going forth with the exercises in this book, I encourage you to implement some version of this process, or whatever technique(s) work for you to bring yourself to a quiet, neutral, centered space, where you can quiet your mind, tune in, and listen. Many of the following exercises in this book require you to come from a merging between this place of meditation and from a place of contemplation.

What I mean by contemplation is to take the question and concentrate your whole being on it, yet without any effort or tension. With contemplation, some gems of novel wisdom will arise (if you allow them). And when they do, allow yourself ample time for the cellular digestion of such a-ha moments—this will help them to become embedded and learned.

In the next section, you will learn how to further access information from specific parts of yourself, putting the above-mentioned techniques into action.

Chapter 2:

The Analyzer, the Heart, and the Third Eye

Notice the thoughts circling through your mind right now. (Pause.)

With your eyes closed, notice, where in your body do the thoughts tend to go?

Do they move fast or slow?

Watch how they move, their density, their intensity.

Is there any movement occurring in your eyes?

Optionally, you can imagine yourself floating out of your body and onto the upper wall or somewhere above yourself. From this third-person perspective, look down at yourself, and watch yourself having thoughts.

Just for now, let's give them permission to be there, realizing they have good intentions.

For most of us, circling thoughts stay stuck in the front of our mind, a region known as the frontal cortex. Logic, analysis, and reasoning come from this area. We'll call this area "the analyzer."

This part of our brain plays a very important role, as we utilize it throughout the day to make all our logical decisions and to keep us safe. When danger is abounded, this part of the brain responds instantly in order to figure out the best escape route or response to take. Thus, it plays a great evolutionary role in helping us to survive.

There's nothing wrong with using our analyzer or frontal cortex throughout our day. Most of us need this part of ourselves to make decisions at work and perform our daily jobs. In fact, using this part of the mind only may become an issue when we allow it to run the show and direct the course of our personal decisions, thoughts, and actions, disregarding the aspects of ourselves that may be better suited to guide us.

Until we learn the "right" role of this part of our body, it can misguide us and get in the way of connecting emotionally with others.

Exercise: The Analyzer and the Center of the Head

Bring all your attention toward the front of your head. If you need help with bringing your attention here, simply perform this math equation: What is 15 X 3?

How does keeping your focus in this region make you feel?

Ask your analyzer if there's anything it wishes to tell you.

Now, release your attention from this area, soften your facial muscles, and next bring your focus a few inches backward toward the center of your head, the region between your two ears. Pay attention to what you notice specifically in your muscles and body, as you focus here.

You might notice an instant softening in the muscles between your eyebrows and around your eyes. And you might perhaps even experience a subtle shift throughout your entire body, as you bring your consciousness away from the analyzer and into the center of your head.

If you feel the muscles around your eyes and face working, do less. (If you go too fast or over-work your muscles while doing so, you might get eye strain or even a headache.) Soften your eyes and face even more. Allow your breathing to be smooth and rhythmic.

What is the information you receive from this place?

Now move your attention back and forth a few times between the center of your head and the front of your head. Do this slowly until you are able to differentiate between the two.

This exercise will help raise your ability to hear the subtle messages that reside inside of you (out of your logical critical mind) and help you to understand where the information is coming from. For the entire next part, as well as most of the practices in this book, it is crucial that you access the information from the center of your head, your heart, or from your body to seek answers. The exercise and example below will help you better understand what I mean by this.

How to Access Information from Your Heart

To access information from your heart, put your left hand onto your heart, and wait until you feel your heartbeat into your hand (pause).

Once you feel your heartbeat, create a loving, nurturing place inside yourself, as if you had a baby's head resting on your chest.

Ask yourself, as if you were speaking to your heart, "What is the information I need at this very moment? What is the information I need to know to be at my highest and best self today?" Pause after each question and wait for the answers to rise up and greet you.

I might also add, having the edges of your lips just slightly turned up can help, especially when your intention is to access your "highest light."

How to Access Your "Higher Self"

After spending some time differentiating the voices from these three parts, I encourage you to next get in touch with your "higher self."

This is a term widely used to describe the Wise and All-Knowing One that resides within each and every one of us. I suggest avoiding getting too hung up on what the literal meaning of this term is. Whether you wish to think of it as the Light within you, your Buddha-nature, or your Inner Guidance center, or whatever term best resonates with you, the important thing is to develop a relationship with this part of yourself and learn how to listen to it for guidance. I believe this part to be the compass withinside each one of us. And when our compass is off, our ships may sail us off-course. This part interacts intimately with our third eye and our heart.

The information we receive could come in one of three main ways:
1. We could visualize it or see it happening in our mind's eye or our imagination.
2. We could sense or feel the answer. This might feel similar to when we have a gut feeling that something in our house, our job, with our family, and so forth just isn't right. Or, when we know 100% without a doubt how right something is!
3. We could hear the answer. Perhaps we'll receive a verbal communication, or some specific words will come to mind. Words can be taken quite literally or metaphorically. Whatever they are, make note of them.

Exercise to Get in Touch with Your Higher Self

To get to know this aspect of yourself, first come to a quiet, introspective space. Soften all your facial muscles and clear your mind of any extraneous thoughts (pause as you take a few deep relaxing breaths).

Then request that your higher self show itself to you, in any way, shape, or form, it wishes to come in. And then pause, as you wait for it to appear.

Notice what area of your body you feel it in, or is it outside of yourself?

Ask it a very simple yes or no question. Do I like it here? Is Shara (replace this with your own name) my name? Do I like spinach? Should I wear the purple skirt today?

From where do these answers come? Do the answers show up more like symbols, feelings, words, emotions, and so forth? Some may experience this aspect of themselves in their heart, some may experience it in their third eye, or some may experience it somewhere in between. Some may even experience it outside the body. And if you're having difficulty experiencing it at all, be patient. Over time, you will!

If you are someone who tends to use your analyzer or thinking mind a lot and struggle with this step, then one tip is to soften your eyes and drop your focus slightly lower (out of the front of your mind).

Practice getting to know what the voice of your higher self looks, sounds, and feels like. I suggest after making initial contact with this part, you begin the practice of asking it questions on a daily basis.

At first, avoid questions that you have a preference or bias for as you may be misguided. For instance, yesterday my husband and I were debating where in Mexico we should travel to. My friend mentioned that San Miguel was amazing and that I would love it there. As she was talking, I felt so compelled to go there. When I asked my higher self, of course, it pointed me in that direction, as it was influenced by the thoughts and beliefs I was already feeling. Yet when my husband and I sat down to look at logistics and the bigger picture the obvious answer was a no.

When we allow our inner guidance center to be biased by the thoughts and feelings we are having in the moment, this can sometimes guide us astray. However, at other times, the body's instinctive feeling of excitement is a true indicator of your body's "Yes" messaging.

Make note of what both feel like. Over time, you will learn to tell the difference between these respective energies. With practice and intention, you will also become better apt at putting your own biases, beliefs, and judgments to the side when gathering such information. You will become your own best healer when, so to speak, you get your own self out of the way.

As you develop a relationship with this part of yourself, my hope is you will begin to trust yourself and your decisions more. This then will help you to improve your self-esteem and confidence with all the choices you make in life.

Your heart is the center of love, the center of your head (also known as your third eye) is the center of your intuition, and your analyzer is the logical processing center. What are the differences in the answers you receive from each of these parts?

I encourage you to get into communication with your analyzer, the center of your head, as well as your heart, this week, as each of these three parts can help guide you tremendously when used appropriately. See the next example for how one might do this.

Each of these parts can be quite useful at different times, yet it takes practice to differentiate the voices of each one, and to deliberately choose which one to hear from.

Example:

Allow me to show you how I may practice accessing information from each of these different parts. I will do this exercise in real-time while in a meditative space.

Question: What is in the highest good for my two-year-old daughter?

Heart: Her continuous whining when she sees me is her way of telling me she wants more Mamma time. Provide her with more quality moments. It's important to hug her/hold her, heart to heart. This helps to ground and still her energy. Really see her and listen to her.

Mind: She wants to be lifted and swung around. This is okay, yet it's also important to set strict parameters and avoid giving in to her whining, for instance, when it's bedtime.

Higher Self: I see her as her highest potential—beauty, life, inspiration. She is so full of life and tends to leave a positive impact on others. Let that be an inspiration for me.

Question: How is your day?

Heart: I feel in flow. The weather is beautiful here. I feel so much inspiration and joy. I'm having a productive morning and that was an amazing fitness class. I'm ready to release any irritation that was created between myself and Frank this morning.

Mind: Stay focused. One thing at a time. You are getting a lot done yet avoid letting your ego get ahead of yourself as you could jinx yourself. Stay grounded! The fitness class was a good work out, yet now time to do a few hours of writing. That will help me to feel more accomplished at the day's end. The day started with an irritation with my husband, yet luckily, I was able to step away from that and enjoy the rest of my day.

Higher Self: The day is going well. Continue to keep your heart and your field open. Balance your energy to avoid crashing in the afternoon. Allow your heart to guide you. Even though your husband may be getting snappy with you, know that's due to external circumstances so have compassion rather than reacting. You know how to place a protective field around you when needed to prevent his irritations from impacting you.

Example with my client Eric:

We began our session with my client (we'll call him Eric) telling me how angry he was at himself for making bed decisions in his financial investments. "I just can't seem to get it right," he stated.

In previous sessions we had discussed that one of his inherit beliefs was that "It's just not going to work out for me. Others may get it, yet not me." He had also previously shared about the unhealthy family dynamics he had with his parents which left him with a feeling of abandonment and the beliefs, "I have to take care of it on my own," "no one is here for me," and "I don't know how...I am lost."

I gave him a few minutes to vent about such topics.

Then I instructed him to drop into his heart. To put his left hand over his heart and wait until he feels his heart beat. Once he felt it, I asked him to create an all loving, nurturing environment right there at his heart.

"Staying connected to this feeling in your heart, Eric can you ask yourself to your heart, what is it you wish to say."

Instantly Eric broke into tears. He was without words for almost a minute as he choked up with tears followed by loud guttural sobs. Then he said, "mom, I miss you."

I encouraged him to continue.

"Mom why couldn't you be there more for me." "I'm sorry I went to the bathroom in my pants mom."

"Your mom was very angry at you for that wasn't she?" I asked.

"Yes," he replied

"How old are you right now," I asked.

"Five."

"Eric, I said. That wasn't your fault…it never was. It's not the job of a 5-year-old to caretake himself. Tell the little 5-year-old, he didn't do anything wrong."

I repeated this last sentence three times as the tears in Eric's eyes continued to flow. I could tell he had been holding onto shame and the feeling of being "bad" from his childhood and because of the enormity of this feeling, he had carried around shame and felt like a bad person his entire adult life.

"What does this little one need right now?" I asked.

"To know there's nothing wrong with him," Eric replied

"That's right," I said as I nodded my head.

"Tell him there's nothing wrong with him. Right now, he needs love and to feel as if he's not all alone and didn't do anything wrong. Let's take a few minutes and just be here with the little one."

We continued the session until the little one felt held, nourished, and supported the way he had always wanted (in Eric's imagination), yet unfortunately had no one there to provide it the way the little one needed at the time. We released his feelings of shame and of being a bad person both in the childhood memory, as well as in his current adult perspective.

We ended the session by replacing this with a feeling of inner peace.

See Workbook exercise #3 and 4 for a longer version of how to provide this sort of inner child healing.

There will be mindfulness and "body wisdom" tips and exercises dispersed throughout this book that will help you to tune in and listen inwardly even more. Yet, for now, we are next going to enter into the world of the pain-body, utilizing the tools and perspectives learned in this chapter.

Chapter 3:

Entering the World of the Pain-Body

A client of mine, Beth, came to me today and said, "My anxiety has increased, I can't decide whether to go to a yoga class or a spin cycle class, I'm mad at myself for sleeping in, and I need to get my resume done, as I'm worried about not having a job. I have become aware of my need to always be on the go. And I have recently weaned off my antidepressant."

It's times like this when we are feeling depressed or anxious, when we're spewing with anxiety, frustration, or angst, that we are unable to release this tumescent or pent-up energy. The energy has to be released one way or another, and if it's not going to be released pleasurably (for example, through dancing, sex, working out, etc.), then it will happen in the most unpleasant of avenues.

When we feel these stirring feelings, we basically have three options. One, well unconsciously give ourselves a heavy negative "stroke" to bring our energy down, which could come in the form of either giving or receiving an insult or physical injury (for example, stubbing our toe) or arguing or fighting with a friend or loved one.

Two, we learn to numb or distract ourselves from the actual feelings at hand. Some of us will self-medicate or resort to alcohol. After all, this is the easy way to cope. Or three, we'll develop techniques and strategies that will help us to consciously cope with these feelings.

When we stop taking pain, anti-anxiety, or antidepressant medication, we are left with a void. Our body is unable to produce the chemicals that such medications provided us and there may be a temporary surge in our cortisol (stress hormone) levels. And the hardest part is, we're then left with the emotions the medications were helping us to mask.

We may attempt to run from, reject, or try to push away the sensations that don't feel so good, yet as the adage goes, "What you resist persists," and with pain, this is the absolute truth. We may even try to distract ourselves from the pain through work, addictions, keeping busy, or any other avoidant behaviors. This may work for a period of time, yet in the end, the pain still remains (even though you may be successful at suppressing it for a period of time).

We could choose healthy options such as attending a yoga class, jogging, meditating, journaling, or talking to a friend. I encourage you to make a list of such activities to do when you're feeling such stuck and circling energy, for when we are feeling stress and duress, our mind switches to the involuntary, shutting down our higher logic and reasoning centers. Hence, it's helpful to already have strategies set in place.

In all our attempts, conscious or unconscious, to stop the uncomfortable feelings inside, the moment we let go of control and resistance, these feelings will shift. This occurs when we allow the sensations to move and reorganize and we surrender to feeling them just as they are, fully and presently. Yet this of course requires discipline.

Nothing remains constant. All sensations change. In all the work I've done with and around pain (whether mental or physical), I've come to conclude that the best way to the other side is through.

To be with what is, free from judgment, shame, or resistance, is a meditative practice, for the moment a story or judgment about the experience enters, the sensation is drowned out.

All sensation is neutral. There are no bad sensations—that is, until we place judgments and meaning on to them, just as a baby or a dog is without judgment as to what she/he sees or smells.

The realm of the body is value-neutral. It has no story and no identification, no good or bad, right or wrong, no judgment or direction, as all of these are the actions of the mind. Though it's easy to judge pain or pleasure as good or bad, if we learn to parse apart the single nuances of how each strand of sensation feels, we can view it from a very different angle.

For your reference, the following words are judgments: beautiful, fancy, pretty, nice, awful, ugly, carefully, correctly, eagerly, easily, irritating, etc. Non-judgment descriptors, if used objectively, are words like fast, slow, radiant, glistening, electric, sparkly, repeatedly, intermittent, thick, thin, heavy, light, dark, dim, soft, prickly, constant, dense, sparse, spacious, hot, freezing, cool, sharp, vibrating, and oscillating.

A Focus on Sensation

When performing the following exercise, I encourage you to simply be with the sensation just as it is, without attempting to change it or tone it down. In a lot of meditations, we may add colors or essential oils, our healing heads, or other such means to calm the mind and relax the body. Although useful at times, these techniques can also be seen as distractions, denying ourselves the opportunity to be with the pure raw sensation of what is. I encourage you to stick with this exercise for the entire 10 minutes simply being with what is (almost as if you were a cave explorer wanting to explore all the subtle nuances of the cave, including the density, color, shape, and all its other unique characteristics).

This exercise can be performed while lying on your back or sitting in a chair. Find a comfortable position where you can sit or lie comfortably for 10 solid minutes. Then set a timer.

If your mind goes into a story at any point during this meditation, stop it immediately, and do your best to return back to your internal world.

If you feel an urge to contract, pull away, or fight, this may be the very area you want to allow more surrender.

This next exercise is a meditation on the sensation of the pain-body. (According to the author, Eckhart Tolle, the term pain-body refers to the old emotional pain we carry around inside of us.) This exercise is geared to be performed during times when you are experiencing physical pain or discomfort. However, if you are experiencing emotional pain without any physical pain, it will still work! After all, all emotional pain always expresses itself through the body. Where in your body do you hold this emotional discomfort? This is the part to focus upon for the next exercise.

This exercise works best if you read it into a voice recorder first. Take sufficient pauses after each question, so that the entire recording spans 10 minutes, start to finish. Give yourself a solid 10 minutes to do nothing but feel.

Then lie down on a couch, place an eye mask over your eyes, and take yourself through the following process:

Exercise: Entering the Inner World of Sensation of the Pain-Body

Begin with the meditative exercise, as explained in the previous chapter, under "Basic Steps to Quiet the Mind and Listen.".

Bring all your attention from the outer world to the inside. Pay attention to the sensations that are occurring for you inside your body.

Connect with what it is you are feeling.

Find the area where you are feeling the most discomfort.

What is the size of the discomfort?

The shape of it?

The color of it?

The intensity?

The thickness?

Is it moving or static?

If it moves, where does the sensation move to?

Is the sensation thick or thin?

Has it changed since you started looking at it?

What is the size of it now?

Stay with the noticing. Allow the organic rise and fall of just what is to occur.

Follow your sensations as they shift and change.

Pause for a few moments. Simply do nothing but feel.

(Pause break).

Begin to engage with this area as if it were a separate self.

Ask it the following questions:

"Do you have a message for me?"

"Why are you here?"

"What do you want me to know?"

Connect with the center of your head.

Ask it: "Is there anything else you wish for me to know?"

Connect with your heart.

Ask it: "Is there anything you wish for me to know?"

Connect with the pain part of your body.

Ask it: "Did I miss anything? Is there anything you wish for me to know?"

Take time to allow each part to fully express itself.

Pause.

How does this area feel now?

What is the color, shape, size, density, intensity, movement pattern, etc., of this region? Has anything changed?

Stay with this experience, surrender to it, validate it for as long as it takes to feel a significant shift.

When you feel complete, take a couple of deep breaths, thank these areas of your body for giving you relevant and useful information, and then slowly begin to emerge from the internal to the external, noticing the chair, bed, or couch you are sitting on, noticing the objects in the room, the clarity of your vision, the softness in your face, and the heightening of your senses.

Once this meditation is complete, see if your pain, discomfort, or feeling state has shifted.

However you choose to perform the meditation, the most crucial step to remember is simply to allow yourself to be with what is. By no means do you have to welcome it, or even think fondly of it. The healing comes from stopping the resistance to what is, quieting the mind, and allowing what will arise to arise.

Many clients of mine report feeling a decrease in their physical as well as their emotional symptoms after performing this exercise.

Going forth, anytime you're feeling discomfort in a part of your body, the "laying on of hands" technique works great, as well. Place your hands over this part, really connect with it. Connect with your higher self and begin to have a conversation as to what truly is going on here.

Before we proceed further, it is important to take a step back to explore where the development of our personal internal ecosystem stems from. To do so, we need to take a journey back in time, back to the place where it all began, our earliest years, when our beliefs, thoughts, ideas, memories, defense mechanisms, and preferences first formed.

Part II

Family Systems

All children want to belong. There is absolutely nothing more painful for a little one than being rejected or separated from his or her family. In the mind of an infant, this need supersedes all others, and when it's not met, it equates to a feeling within the child equivalent to death.

For that reason, when we're born, we will do whatever is possible to belong in our family system, to the extent that in a family of thieves, it's the child who doesn't steal who is the guilty one and will grow up paying the pain and consequences of not belonging.

Chapter 4:

Our Longing to Belong

This need to "belong" begins at birth and lasts throughout life. He/she will learn the coded "norms" and what is right versus wrong by what is modeled around him/her.

Think back to your first days of grade school when you learned from your teachers and schoolmates how to act, play, and be. As you continued through grade school, can you remember to what degree you wanted to be liked and included and how you may have shifted your behaviors accordingly?

Yet, nothing overrides the need to belong for a young child to his family of origin. Upon hearing this, your first instinctual thought may be to reject or deny this concept. You may feel that your mom or dad had traits such as manipulation, control, and cruelty that you would never want to repeat. "I would never raise a child the way they raised me."

However, embedded deep in our neural code, the longing and desire for love and connection runs so deep that it affects every nerve and cell of an infant's and young child's body. Every twitch and flutter of the physical body in sync with our need to belong.

When you were an infant, you had no idea of what love truly was. And with your newly developing cerebral cortex, you experienced the world solely through felt experience. You felt the world before you intellectualized it. That is to say, your subconscious mind linked any association of love to what home felt like.

If being with Mom and Dad equals frequent arguments and yelling, and Mom and Dad equal love, then frequent arguments and yelling equals love.

Love=Mom & Dad / Mom & Dad=fighting / Love=Fighting

This connection will quickly be encoded and linked in the mind of the little one, and will remain there, tucked away in the subconscious as he or she ages.

Children are born loving their parents and whatever version of love they received as a child was how they encoded the word love in life. This means that if your home felt like chaos, loneliness, and confusion, with unavailable parents, then that is how you coded the words love, home, and family.

As adults, we may wonder why finding a healthy relationship is so difficult, when in reality, our subconscious continues playing out the same strategies we once adopted as a child as a means to find love.

The mind keeps a fascinating Rolodex of memories of what love is, and it will link any association of love to what home felt like growing up. If love equals home and home equals abandonment, then love equals abandonment.

Abandonment may not mean that Mother or Father actually left the home. It may mean that both Mom and Dad were there, yet they just were unable to "see" or be emotionally available for you. (If this is the case, from the opposite-sex parent, as you age, you might find your love attraction to be with a partner who is either physically or emotionally unavailable.)

The reality is we may spend our years looking to find a mate who will heal the unmet needs and wounds we received in childhood (more frequently, the opposite-sex parent), thinking maybe if I act or behave the "right" way, then he'll see me and become available for me or see how lovable or worthy I am. Yet the unfortunate truth is that more likely than not, the same pattern that you had with dad (or a parent) will soon reveal itself, adding even more salt to the original wound…unless this original need is met prior to meeting your partner!

This inherit need to "belong" to the family system becomes embedded in one's earliest years, and we will go so far as to take on the burden of responsibility and guilt or whatever weighs heavy on the family as a means to be a part of their collective consciousness.

As we grow, we may begin to develop beliefs that differ from those of our family. By the time we reach adolescence, we may reject some of the family dynamics, traits, and beliefs in order to build what we believe to be a healthy separate life.

We may experience rebellion or denial as our identity forms and may even physically move away from our family in an attempt to "disentangle" ourselves from "their stuff." Yet the sinking truth is that until the family wounds are healed, they will follow us no matter where we go. They will follow us because they are in us! They are deep in our neural code.

The ability to sprout fresh neural connections and recode our meaning of love, safety and belonging becomes more difficult the older we get. The younger we are, are brains are more "plastic" or changeable. While the older we get, a brain's plasticity decreases as the lower parts of the brain (brainstem and cerebellum) become less flexible than the higher parts (limbic and cortex) to change.

However, with the new body of research on neuroplasticity, we now know that we do have the ability to rewire old neural pathways at any age and step into the loving partnership and the life we so desire!

Memetics & Family Traits

When we are born into a family, we inherit not only our biological genes, but also so many of the beliefs, behaviors, and habits of our family. They were passed on genetically and without will throughout the generations. This concept is also known as "memetics."

The concept of memetics first originated with Darwinian evolution and was further expanded upon by the German psychotherapist, Burt Hellinger and the scientist, Richard Dawkins, in his 1976 book, The Selfish Gene. Memetics equates to the genetic code of the emotional traits, habits, skills, beliefs, behaviors, or information passed on from generation to generation; in a sense, it is a cultural or familial transmission. As with genetics, it's possible for a meme, or a trait, to skip generations.

We see it all the time, sad father, sad son, alcoholic mother, alcoholic daughter, insecure father, insecure son, infidelity in father, infidelity in son, etc. Relationship difficulties and emotional hardships of the parents are often mirrored, repeated, and lived out by the children.

It is true that we develop much of our traits and characteristics through modeling and mirroring our caregivers, yet I'm going to focus the scope of this conversation solely upon the inheritance of memetic traits.

For family systems where judgment and criticism are the norms, the parents criticize the child, the children criticize each other, and pretty soon, the child ends up feeling "safe" with criticism. Or maybe the father is very domineering and controlling and often scolds the mother. And the mother reacts with submission or apology and seeks to hide from him.

In situations like this, the child may "memetically" adopt similar patterns that mirror one parent more than the other, depending on the child's gender, birth order with other siblings, and a host of other factors. Or he/she may adopt a consolidation of the characteristics of both parents or just the flip opposite. An example of the opposite trait would be a controlling confident mother and a shy and submissive daughter.

In unhealthy family systems, a child takes on too heavy a burden of their family's suffering, which wasn't dealt with "upstream" or in generations prior. This, in many cases, results in years down the road in some sort of diagnosis or pain state.

Whew, that's a lot!

We will address this concept of memes further in the exercise below, yet for now, I'm going to pause here in this conversation, for if you have children, you might be thinking about what "suffering" you have passed on to your child or children. We can all learn to be better parents, while at the same time, we can never protect our children from all the negative emotions and traumas they will face throughout life, for, in a nutshell, this is their journey.

Only growth and learning come from every experience, and as we'll learn later on in this book, that it's our greatest hardships and our "adversaries" (as we'll call them) that strengthen us and teach us the essential lessons of our life's Journey.

If you are a parent who experienced a great deal of grief, sadness, misery, anger, or loss while raising a young child, the worst thing you could do is punish yourself. We are all learning how to traverse through this wild and wily universe together, using all of the resources we have at hand. And I trust that we as parents are doing the best we know how to raise our children in positive, loving environments.

Pain and hardship are a human experience, and no humans are exempt from it, for with it comes expansion and growth, which I believe is the true plight of the human race. The faster we are able to learn the lessons each experience brings us, the faster we will grow (I believe).

If you are a parent, it's never too late to begin the practice of tuning in to your child's individual emotional and physical needs and do whatever it takes to help him/her meet those needs. And, here's a little secret. Most likely the unmet needs your child is currently coping with are the same ones as they were dealing with in their first five years of life.

Exercise to Recognize and Release Family Memes

Memes may include loneliness, husband/men who go suddenly crazy on you, history of abortions, anger, frustration, feelings of unworthiness, difficulty getting jobs, difficulty keeping a mate in your life, inability to have fun until all the work is done, hiding the real hurt and pain, finding relationships where you are the one taking care of your partner, believing who I am is what I do (hence, I need to work hard to prove who I am in love or relationships), alcoholic partners, isolation, settling for a life that is unsatisfactory, working extremely hard at a job that is unfulfilling, difficulty making money, difficulty keeping the money you make, being a victim of abuse, supervisors/superiors who feel threatened by you, and hence, silence your voice, being overpowered by others, etc.

Do any of these traits resonate with you? In this exercise, I invite you to look at your life, recognize your characteristics, and release your inherited memes that are no longer serving you.

Balcony Exercise to Release Family Memes and Ancestral Patterns

First, make a list of the memes you struggle with today.

Then imagine a huge amphitheater the size of a football field. You are standing just below the first bleacher. As you turn around, you see your parents standing on the bleacher behind you looking down upon you with unconditional eyes, your mom, on the left, and your father, on the right.

Behind them are their parents (your four grandparents), behind them are their parents (your eight great-grandparents), behind them...continue filling the amphitheater as full as you can get it, welcoming all your ancestors who came before you. As you turn around and look directly at all of your predecessors, see if you can get any information about how these traits may have been present within them.

Begin with the first item from this list.

Ask your higher self, which side of your family did this trait stem from? Your mother's, your father's, or both?

Ask the family members who passed this trait on to you to light up like a light bulb to reveal themselves.

Pause.

Then I want you to turn (in your imagination) toward the participants on this side of the balcony and see them experiencing such pain (for instance, control, shame, killer instinct, etc.).

Recognize it's not your fault you have had to carry the weight of this pain, rather it's the familial imprints that were passed your way. And with that, you turn to them and say out loud, "The buck stops here! I give you back your pain."

Then envision yourself removing this trait from your own physical body and giving this trait back to them. You could envision it as the collective "them" or an individual person.

Pause. Take time with this. Knowing that no parent truly wishes to impart harm upon their child, but rather, feels the familial obligation to take back what is theirs. By doing this, you are in no way imparting further harm upon them, as this trait is already present within them. Rather, by releasing this trait inside of yourself, the effects of that will then trickle upstream to them.

When you complete this step to your satisfaction, check in to see if there are other traits, or memes, that you have taken on that you are now ready to let go of, remembering that all memes always originate from someone else and were passed down on to you and it is your rightful duty to give them back.

If so, repeat the process above.

Stick with it for as long as it takes until you feel a sense of resolution and peace.

Next, turn your back to the balcony and look only forward. Feel the lightness and spaciousness fill your body in the space where this trait(s) once was.

Pause.

Imagine your parents now putting their hands on your shoulders, in support of you. Imagine their parents placing their hands upon their shoulders, in support of them, to send to you, and all the generations prior placing their hands upon their children, all in support of you, sending a streaming line of energy in your direction.

Imagine leaning back into your parents' four hands. Feel the support of all the generations that stand before you, all sending their love and support downstream toward you.

Pause.

Feel the rivers of energy flowing your way. Breathe it in. Your heart is pumping. Let whatever emotions wish to arise to arise.

Proclaim out loud, "Now I take life in its fullness from you."

Feel the heat from all the previous generation's hands being transferred on to you (despite the fact that you might be feeling a chill in your body).

And then, when you are ready, open your eyes and look forward. Look forward toward the infinite potential that lies ahead, toward the possibilities and new opportunities that await.

The last step is to give gratitude—gratitude to all the previous generations that tilled the soil and endured a great deal of suffering, pain, and persecution, all the ones who fought and survived long enough to contribute toward your very existence.

When you are ready, I'd like you to stand back up (either literally or in your imagination), and turn one last time toward your ancestors, all with their eyes and prayers being placed on you, and say, "Thank you. Thank you for my life!"

Where Does Such Suffering Come From?

Most people these days believe it's necessary to make an effort and suffer at least to some degree to succeed.

Yet, from an ancestral point of view, where might such suffering stem from?

Perhaps it's our maternal line that endured a lifetime of submission, subordination, and being controlled by husbands who they never truly loved. Or from our father's lineage, the pressure to hold our emotions in, toughen ourselves, and take the hard blows.

It comes as no surprise that so many people are contracting ailments of unknown origin, for when such long-standing ancestral wounds remain unhealed, they will eventually be expressed somatically throughout the body in one or more of the family members.

If, for instance, if a family member is lost or pushed out, i.e. due to a miscarriage, death, or simply due to the parents inability to care for their child or some unacceptable quality they exhibited, (i.e. perhaps a member is gay, marrying a person of a different race or color, or sent off to a boarding school as a child due to the parents inability to raise the child), we may experience a painful hole in our heart; he fabric of the family field is now torn and reparations will be necessary for us to heal.

As they leave, it may feel as if a part of ourselves has departed with them, and life will never be the same.

I once had a client (Monica) who suffered from lung and respiratory symptoms as well as depression of unknown cause. I led her and a small group of her friends through a family constellation session (a process developed by the psychologist, Bert Hellinger, to free the subconscious wounding or entanglements of a family system).

A family is an energy field. Where there is damage or trauma in any particular part of your ancestry, often later generations end up paying the price for what current and past generations didn't fully resolve. Each member of a family system is part of an interconnected web, and when any member of the web is rejected, abdicated, or separated from their family (for instance, an early death, murder, being gay in a biased family, etc.), it has a deep impact upon the whole of the web.

The goal of family constellations work is to heal such entanglements and mend the field of the family, for when left unhealed, certain members of the family "downstream" will pay the price.

This particular constellation session focused on the entanglements of Monica's grandfather. There were eight participants who took part in this constellation, each acting as a "representative" for a specific member of

Monica's family who played an important role in this particular entanglement.

The story goes as follows: Monica's uncle had stolen all the family's inheritance from her grandfather and her grandfather felt deceit and anger and died feeling so much anger and hurt from being taken advantage of.

Even though the basic facts of this story were known prior to the constellation, through this process, the enormity of Monica's grandfather's pain was felt, witnessed, and eventually released. This then had a rippling effect, impacting all the family members who were being "represented" in this particular constellation. Subjectively, this was experienced by participants experiencing things such as tears and then relief, a sudden onset of back pain, followed by an easing of it, an increase in the feeling of anger and rage in the one participant who represented her grandfather followed by a feeling of deeper understanding and support coming from some of the other family members. We finally came to a space of unity, love, and resolution, as the constellation came to completion.

Family constellations can be quite powerful at healing the subconscious energetic wounds of a family system, which, in the end, can resolve mysterious diseases, physical and emotional pain, and unwanted patterns (such as abuse, rejection, and difficulty attracting a mate).

I reconnected with Monica one week after this process was complete and she stated that her respiratory and throat issues had lessened. She had the stark realization that she had been holding the burden and suffering of her grandfather, even though she only had known him as a very young child.

In fact, she had only known her grandfather until the age of three, when he passed. Although her memories of him were almost nonexistent, the energetic cords or memes appeared to have been passed on to her. Family traits, or memes, can very likely skip a generation.

Which memes, or traits, get passed on through the generations happens without rhyme or reason. Instead, they are tied to an individual's soul contracts, which he or she made prior to choosing to take a body in this lifetime.

This might also explain why some of us may have phobias of unknown origin such as an exorbitant fear of snakes or of being submersed in an open body of water.

Some of the emotions and physiological reactions we experience in our own physical bodies may not make sense at the moment until we begin to understand them in the light of this novel perspective.

The DNA of the emotional body is passed through the morphogenic field through our lineage lines onto us. (A morphogenic field is an invisible organization of wave particles that have an inherited collective memory from all previous things of its kind. It consists of cells, molecules, atoms, etc., that respond to biochemical signals in the "field." Think of a flock of birds or a school of fish, how they remain so close to one another as they fly or swim and know just when and which direction to turn in synchrony. This is what we may term a "field phenomena" where an invisible communication occurs, similar to how telepathy might work.)

What this means is that simply by being born into a family a pure innocent young child inherits not only the DNA sequencing, but also all of the energies of previous generations have potential to be transferred through the bloodlines downstream onto them. A child becomes an integral part of the field (even as early as in utero), receiving and transmitting a confluence of information, even to members of the family he or she has never seen or met. However, the field phenomena tends to be strongest with your immediate family and those who are still alive and closest to you.

Suffering Obligation of Love

This unconscious contract, referred to as "The Suffering Obligation of Love," goes something like this: "Mom, I don't want you to suffer. Hence, I'll take on the pain so that you don't have to suffer." And then the suffering is passed "downstream."

Some children feel a heavier obligation to take on the family's suffering & pain (they are more empathic), while others are benign. When a child takes on too heavy a burden of their family's suffering (often in unhealthy family systems), this can result years down the road in chronic pain.

What we need to realize is that this obligation truly isn't ours to hold and with conscious practice (such as family constellations and ancestral healing work), we can set ourselves free of these subconscious contracts.

It is our souls that bind us into such contracts, in the first place, and at any time, we have the opportunity to take up our pens and rewrite such agreements.

Chapter 5:

Guilt and Sin, Good and Bad

On our journey through the pain-body as discussed in chapter 2, we naturally have a tendency to judge certain sensations as "bad" and other ones as "good." And when we're in pain, the tendency is to discard or to disassociate with our physical bodies, especially when the pain becomes too much, hence, further reinforcing the concept of the term "bad."

Yet what if just the opposite were true, that the "bad" sensations are simply sending out a message that something in the system is off-balance and in need of fine-tuning? And it's what we deem as "bad" that may be the very thing now standing in the road of our greatest desires.

Along with each twinge of the "bad" feeling inside, there is always a correlated belief that is associated with it. Dig deep and you'll find it. You wouldn't feel the "bad" sensations if you didn't have negative thoughts about yourself somewhere, somehow. And it's this belief that's causing a contraction or a tightening, a resistance to what is, which then draws us further away from our desires.

Growing up, we developed an individuated rule book for ourselves of right vs. wrong, good vs. bad. Our entire life, we've wanted to be a "good" person, and avoid the "bad." Growing up, perhaps in your family, accomplishment and achievement was considered in the "good" category, while playing and frivolous activities were placed into the "bad." Or maybe you learned that expressing joy and happiness by shouting, laughing, and romping freely around the house would bring you punishment, but if you became quiet and well-behaved, then you would be rewarded.

One of my clients, Michelle, has a desire to make more money. When asked the question, "What about making money is so bad?" We found deep subconscious beliefs around how money equated to effort and self-sacrifice. A part of her believed that those who made money easily were in some way undeserving. And another part of her had judgments around people who had money categorizing them as righteous or self-serving.

What this means is that, for Michelle, making money comes with cross motivations, for if making more money equals suffering and effort, or if making money means I'm one of "them," then maybe making money is not what I really want.

Pause right now and ask yourself what it is that you want in your life.

Then, make a list of all the little voices you have within yourself that are telling you that having that thing is wrong or bad. Is some subconscious aspect of yourself in contradiction to you having it?

(Reflection break.)

The aspect of good and bad, guilt and sin has been ingrained in our civilization since the beginning of recorded history. Yet we only have to go back to our own childhood to assess how this concept may have been true for us, for, as a young child, when we did something "bad," we were punished. That experience imprinted within us the belief that "when we are bad, we deserve punishment."

Then, after the punishment and guilt were administered, you eventually got to be in the "good" category once again. Your entire moral life since this time has been based on being a "good" daughter, son, friend, partner, parent, and overall, a "good" person. We have formed, by now, a long list of criteria describing our idealized compendium of behaviors that makes a person "good." We have learned to stow away, hide, and reject the "bad," welcoming only the "good."

It's an evolutionary trait passed on throughout the centuries to believe self-sacrifice, pain, and punishment are all part of the pathway to being "good." After all, throughout the centuries, our ancestors endured generation after generation of strong religious and governmental programming that imposed laws of good and evil, promoted sacrifice and suffering, and ingrained people with a black-and-white moral code of right versus wrong. Somewhere in our socialization process our wires got crossed thinking enduring punishment is the pathway to being good and happy, and enjoying ourselves is bad and undeserving.

I encourage you to reflect inwardly as to if even an ounce of such a notion might be true for you.

The Victim-Perpetrator Relationships

One of the clearest examples of this is in victim-perpetrator relationships, as it's always the victim who comes out looking like the good and innocent one, while the abuser or perpetrator gets put into the "bad" category when in reality, the victim can't exist without the perpetrator. It's a symbiotic relationship, where one needs the other in order to provide a sense of identity or purpose that they so desire.

It's difficult to explain this concept, for it is without physical or material form (which is how humans in their three-dimensional reality perceive and come to understand things). Yet if I were to take this etheric concept and find an analogous way of describing it in the physical dimension, I may describe it like this:

Let's say all the billions of cells throughout your body align a particular way for every single aspect of who you are. This cellular alignment is influenced through the filters of your life experiences, genetics, biases, beliefs, environmental influences, and the people closest to you. Most of this was encoded for you in your earliest years of life and may very well dictate what it is you will attract or repel.

Every cell in your body attracts, repels, or is neutral toward that which it interacts with. For instance, around certain people, we may tend to lean closer in towards, while other people we lean away from. This mostly occurs at an ethereal cellular level or beyond what the human eye can perceive. In general, the nervous system veers toward safety, comfort, and the familiar, and away from danger and the unknown.

Here's an example: Let's say a girl, we'll call her Sara, was abused physically as a child. Now, as a 34-year-old woman, she is out in the world, looking for love. She meets a beautiful man and falls in love, only to find, within a few months, he starts to be cruel to her.

As a young girl she encoded the feeling she had with this "type" of man as "familiar" and "home" (despite how much she despised being treated the way). She might even find a man with a completely different demeanor as her father, yet in the long run, the feeling she is left with on the inside is quite similar. She becomes the victim in this story.

As most of us journey to find our love mate, we cannot help but recreate the same patterns that we witnessed and experienced in youth. For our nervous systems keep a detailed map. We are constantly taking in information through our sensory world; what we see, hear, feel, taste and touch then informs our behaviors, physiology, and emotions. All of the experiences around us and the people with whom we interact have an effect on our internal world.

Every fear impulse, every twinge of contraction in our muscles sends off a cascade of neural impulses and chemical signals which communicate with all other parts of ourselves. The body keeps a fascinating memory (or imprint) of such states. The more frequent emotional and physiological states occur, as well as the more intense they are, the deeper they become imprinted (this is true for both positive and negative emotional states).

What this means is that Sara's pattern of attracting men who are bad to her will most likely continue to exist until she heals the wounds at a deep cellular level. This will require her to alter her physiological and emotional reactions to previous fears and triggers. Difficult as this is, it is very possible to do!

Anytime a pattern exists in your life where you find yourself a victim, it may be reflexive to feel anger, blame, resentment, and pain. Yet we must eventually look beyond these emotions to understand the "why" we are the attractor of such elements. What "karma" in this lifetime or past, what ancestral wounding, what traumas or limiting beliefs are still in need of healing? And what steps do we then need to take to heal such inner wounds?

After all, these are the cards we have been handed in this lifetime. And even though the Ole Mighty One may not have delivered the cards fairly, we DO have the possibility of evoking change and attracting an entirely different set of circumstances.

Just looking at life from this perspective allows us not only to begin taking a more responsible stance; it also creates the possibilities for altering the people, places, and things we attract.

This is the secret key to living a happy life!

Part III

Physiology, Beliefs, and Emotions

All our emotions and beliefs have an effect on our movement patterns, mannerisms, and physiological states. They impact everything from how smoothly our eyeballs glide in our eye sockets and how heavily our down step is in walking to the tone and volume of our voice.

All emotions have an associated response in the cells of our muscles, joints, organs, and bones. And the converse is true as well, meaning that our physiological states have a direct impact upon our emotions. With this notion as a starting point, it becomes easier to see how the mind and the body (from a cellular perspective) act as one.

Chapter 6:

Effects of Negative Thinking

Self-negating thoughts such as I'm not good enough repeated enough times will color the landscape of our minds, molding us to believe it is true. This negative landscaping hinders our progression and can petrify into a homeostasis. Eventually, we succumb to the attitude that this is who we are, narrowing and dirtying the lens through which we perceive opportunity, career, and love.

When we are unable to hear our deep inner wisdom and rather allow our unconscious mental chatter to run the show, we condemn our physical selves to suffer, and that suffering occurs on a very conscious level.

Negative Self-Talk and Its Effects upon the Body

Most people are completely unaware of all the self-negating thoughts that run in the subconscious 24/7: You should be on time, you messed up again, you had an opportunity, and once again, you sabotaged it, self-talk like that. Yet every time any negative thought occurs, it causes constriction and tightness in specific parts of the body.

Self-negating thoughts that have to do with feeling lost and confused, thoughts like I don't know what to do, it's all up to me, I should be making something of myself, I just can't figure out what, etc., will be lodged more in the throat and head region (and may, over time, result in headaches or dizziness).

People who tend to believe they need to effort in life to succeed, life is an uphill battle, or I need to put more of myself into things, will most likely have some degree of tension around their jaw, toes, buttocks, the muscles between each of their eyebrows and eyes, and more of their weight will be distributed forward towards their toes and the front side of themselves. Their nose and head will most often be located in front of their toes rather than on top of their spine.

Thoughts that feel like more of a punch in the stomach such as I f*cked up again or I don't deserve will result in tightness and a "pulling-in" sensation in their throats and abdominal region.

Feelings of being trapped in one's circumstances, thoughts like I'll never get ahead, life is a struggle (bills, finances, long work hours, lack of personal time, etc.) or I can't get away, will result in constriction around the throat and ribs/chest area. This person will very likely have extremely restricted breathing and it may feel as if the walls are caving in on them.

People who feel like they need to protect their energy and set a boundary around themselves to prevent others from taking more than their fair share of them (due to their history of people wanting more of them then they are able to give), will struggle with throat and chest tightness as they pull in their breathe and harden their upper ribs as if to say "STOP." They will also over contract their neck extensors and have a more rigid and straight neck or cervical spine. This is a self-protective stance to block others from coming in. (See Boundaries chapter in the workbook.)

In the words of Feldenkrais trainer, Dr. Jeff Haller, "Our neurosis is inhibited in our muscular habit."

Any chronically negative thought patterns will eventually lead to chronic muscular tension, which then if provoked enough, can eventually lead to chronic pain and disease. All negative thoughts are constricting; all positive thoughts are expansive.

Let's put this notion into theory. For the next exercise, we'll experiment with how both positive and negative beliefs affect our posture and gait.

Thinking, Walking Exercise

Try standing up and thinking these thoughts: I need to make an effort in life, and life is an uphill battle.

Take on these beliefs completely. Think about putting in more effort and struggle, then see how this affects your standing posture and gait.

Now let those thoughts go, invite in a balanced rhythmic breath, align your head over your toes, and think the thoughts: Right here is just where I need to be. Life is full of joy and ease.

See how these thoughts now affect your standing posture. Walk around the room and compare the difference in how each of these thoughts affects your movements.

(Please see the accompanying workbook for more in-depth exercises on stopping the monkey mind of negative thinking and altering limiting beliefs.)

All of our thoughts and emotions have a direct impact on our balance, physiology, and gait, and just the contrary is true, as well. As we improve the state of our mind, we improve the state of our body.

> "Movement is life. Life is a process. Improve the quality of the process and you improve the quality of life itself."
>
> —*Moshe Feldenkrais*

Chapter 7:

Muscular States of Emotions

All our thoughts, beliefs, and emotions have an effect on our physical composure and muscular states of contraction, which then impacts the overall state of our health.

Chronic shame, for instance, and feelings of unworthiness result in the head stooping down, shortening of the neck, rounding of the back, and a pulling inward of the extremities as if to hide and protect the abdomen and chest.

This may also result in more contraction of the muscles surrounding the trachea (where air and sound waves travel from the nose and mouth into your lungs). Vocal pitch is therefore softened and comes from the back of the throat rather than from the diaphragm and lower body.

When it comes to the act of sex, men could have erectile dysfunction issues and woman may struggle with the feeling of "not deserving to have pleasure" and have difficulty orgasming and the like.

Chronic fear of what is to come, in which one feels the need to be on high alert, causes the eyelids to open wider, the neck and back of the head to pull back and stiffen, the shoulder blades to flatten (or in some cases to flair), the low-back muscles to contract, and breathing to be inhibited. This person's movements may be quicker, sharper, and more impulsive. Their arms may be held more tightly by their sides, especially as they walk and their legs are held closer together as they unconsciously overwork their inner thighs.

They may also have raised upper trapezius (shoulders), rigidity in their joints, tightness of the jaw, back, shoulders, and neck, especially the posterior neck muscles. This could over time lead to radiating pain. They may have difficulty shutting off this part of their mind long enough to enjoy or even open to the act of sex (if they are a female).

Lack of trust holds a similar physiological state (as chronic fear) in which one's stance is more guarded, almost as if they are creating an energetic wall or barricade around themselves (and their heart) that prevents others from entering. This also shows up in their auric field, as they bring their energy fields in closer toward their body.

Those who over-think their next move or second-guess themselves may have the same guarded posture as just described. These people may fear losing themselves in intimacy and hence become people-pleasers, conforming to the needs and likes of others, and then eventually pulling back.

Their thoughts may circulate in the forefront of their mind, as they think and over-think their actions and words. Over time, this could result in headaches or eye strain, pain in the neck, hips, hand, wrist, or a multitude of other places.

Chronic pressure to be good enough and to live up to perfectionist ideals can result in a stiff and erect upper torso, inhibited chest breathing, and a tightness around their inner thighs and buttocks (similar to the urgency pattern, as described below).

Over a period of time, this will eventually cause the inward curve of the neck and the low back to straighten, the upper chest and sternum region to protrude forward and upward, and the ribcage to tighten.

These people are often good orators and are precise in the choice of words they use to communicate. All the while, they may be more reactive to events on the outside and beat themselves up for little mistakes. They may hold their head high with vigilance in their eyes and presence in their demeanor.

They may be more prone to have minor aches and pains throughout their bodies, which they heed little attention to.

Chronic thoughts and behaviors associated with urgency, anxiety, or scarcity may result in constriction around the throat and chest region with short, fast, and possibly labored breathing, and they may walk with a jerky, short, and fast gait with their legs held close towards one another. Their anus, gluteal muscles and leg adductors (inner thighs) will be held tightly.

This person may hold the belief that effort and hard work equals success, and hence, he or she needs to keep putting pressure upon him or herself to do and accomplish more. Although this person might be proficient in sports such as running, tasks that require more eye/hand motor coordination and balance might be more challenging.

Their range of motion may be more limited, especially in their neck, back, arms, and legs. They may be the ones who find a yoga class challenging due to their lack of flexibility, or they may have less ease with looking out of the rearview window when driving.

Over time, this pattern could result in asthma, insomnia, neck and back pain, thyroid issues, eating disorders, and digestive, prostate, and urinary issues (just to name a few).

Chronic worry, whether around finances, career, home life, family, health concerns, etc., can result in difficulty breathing, sleep apnea, and other heart conditions, as well as back pain, infertility, digestive issues, breast cancer, and so much more. Worry causes muscles to contract inward, which may eventually impinge on nerves and arteries.

Chronic obligations and responsibilities may result in tightening of the neck extensors, while hardening and freezing the rib and chest region in attempts to hold vulnerability and emotions inside (so their focus can then be directed more outside of themselves). These people are constantly thinking about what they "should" be doing for others and beating themselves up when they fall short. They may feel guilty when spending time and money on themselves and may experience more joy when giving gifts to others.

When looking to find a romantic partner, this will become an issue. Putting continual focus and attention on others' needs may work for the initial period, yet there will come a time when this woman will come to the realization that she wants to be the one seen and attended to and she's tired of being the emotional caretaker.

Women sometimes tend to gain a few extra pounds in order to create extra space in their bodies to hold all the emotions and responsibility, while other women may maintain a thin frame due to their subconscious need to keep busy and accomplish things (and avoid feeling). They may deny themselves pleasure, be it in the form of food, compliments, or even sexual pleasure (or receive it in binges).

The third category of body types has to do with putting very little attention on food and diet, as they learned from a young age that their focus needed to be elsewhere, on more survival sort of topics. These people may need to make a conscious effort to really even taste food and appreciate the distinct flavors.

If one is unable to break this pattern of frequently feeling obligation and responsibility for the world around you, this could eventually lead to conditions of the heart, headaches, obesity, irritability (suppressed and held in until the pressure explodes), high blood pressure, low or mid back pain, feet, knee, or lower-body issues, chronic fatigue, thyroid issues, fibroids, cysts, endometriosis, mold toxicity, and fibromyalgia.

Chronically feeling inadequate (often stemming from feeling subjugated and separated from your peer groups in childhood) will lead to a composure (developed over the years) to hide such inadequacies. Depending on their circumstances, this can be reflected in one of three ways:

One, they may walk with a puffed-out chest, bringing the low back forward, the head and shoulders pulled back, walking on their heels, with toes pointed outward, giving the facade that everything is a-okay in here. This is common in people who tend to be short (or may have other physical characteristics that they may have interpreted as "less than"), as this posture may subconsciously make them feel bigger and more important. As these folks age, they may learn to lead with their assets and guard or hide the rest, which includes hardening or suppressing emotions. Over time, this posture can result in low-back and neck pain.

Two, this belief can result in postures closer to the shame tendencies (as mentioned above).

Or, three, a combination of both patterns.

Our Posture as a Culmination of Our Life Experiences

Our thoughts and beliefs about ourselves and the world around us began forming in our first few years of life. They influenced the shape, structure, and approximations between our bones, muscles, tendons, joints, and ligaments. By the time we're adults, the way we hold our head and shoulders, the degree to which our shoulder blades flair off our back, the tightness of our anal sphincter, the rounding of our spine, our breathing patterns, etc., have already become established.

There's no physical therapist or chiropractor who can say, "Hold your diaphragm in and your head up high," who can change that.

Our postures are a culmination of our life experiences, and the only way to change such a disposition is through one of two ways:

1. Change the way you feel on the inside (by altering your thoughts, beliefs, and emotions).

2. Change your physiological and muscular states.

The good news is that when you change either one of these two components, it automatically changes the other. Healing is most effective when you address it from both ends!

A helpful suggestion is the next time you find yourself stuck in a negative spiral, try holding your chin up and your shoulders back. And then find something…anything to smile about.

If you have a pet, a child, or a beautiful plant, it makes finding a reason to smile easier. Then see if your emotional and physiological states shift.

Healing through the Emotional Body

Beneath all chronic pain lies unresolved or unhealed emotions. Emotions such as anger, resentment, sadness, and remorse when held on to for long enough can eventually express themselves somatically through the physical body in the form of physical ailments and pain.

Ideally, we want to work through such emotional states and eventually come to a place of acceptance, gratitude, and love, for it is with these three ingredients that true healing comes.

In my workbook, I have several exercises that will help you with just this! I highly encourage you to pause on the reading of this book and work through the exercises "Moving Through the Emotional Body," and "Withholds."

Chapter 8:

Thoughts and Beliefs

Your beliefs and thoughts color and shape the reality of your life. If you believe "Nobody loves me," you will detract people from loving you. If you believe you are lovable, you will attract love. It is a universal law that whatever we place our attention upon grows.

When we focus on the negative circumstances of our lives, we will attract even more circumstances that validate these beliefs and feelings. Your outer experiences are merely a reflection of your inner world. The words we speak, the thoughts we think, the beliefs we have, are all, in this very moment, shaping the present and future YOU!

It is a universal principle that like attracts like and the more we stay stuck in negative beliefs and thought patterns, it attracts those concordant experiences our way. Anytime a limiting belief is present, the universe responds by providing correlated life circumstances, which then provide even more ample evidence to support the pre-existing belief.

In other words, we create for ourselves a world consistent with our thoughts and beliefs, potentially blocking the very outcome that we wish to create. Hence, it's important to pluck those prickly weeds (negative beliefs) that we have sown for too long. These will often be growing in places where they strangle out money, health, love, intimacy, and everything else we wish to thrive.

You will next be guided through a number of processes that can help unravel negative thought patterns and beliefs (some you will find in the accompanying workbook).

Yet, the first step is to really identify and make a list of what is at the root of our feelings, thoughts, and beliefs. After all, we've been pruning the surface for long enough. You'll know you've found a root belief when it lands with a *thunk* or a feeling of contraction inside of you.

Core beliefs sound like a variation of the following:

I'm not good enough.

I'm not pretty enough.

I'm lazy.

I'm unlovable.

I'm separate.

I'm unworthy.

I don't belong.

I'm on the outside.

I'm different.

I don't matter.

I'm damaged.

I'm a failure.

I am too much.

I'm insignificant.

Nobody likes me.

Something is wrong with me.

Life is overwhelming.

I can't do it on my own.

I'm a fraud.

Exercise to Retrain Our Body's Physiology during Negative Thoughts and Beliefs

It is recommended to first record this meditation into a voice recorder, leaving ample time and space for reflection between each question, and then sit or lie back in a relaxed and meditative space to listen as you replay the recording.

1. Decide what the limiting belief you would like to work with is from the list above (or make up your own).

2. Imagine a time when you experienced this belief. Enter into that experience in your imagination. Allow yourself to feel this limiting belief completely. (Discomfort will indeed arise, yet I encourage you to do your best to be with it. Try to let the uncomfortable sensations radiate through every cell and pore of your body, as you did in the prior exercises, rather than push them away).

3. Notice how your body presents itself when feeling this way. Use this list as your guide. Do your best to refrain from any judgment.
   What is happening in your:
   Breathing?
   Jaw and teeth?
   Fingers and toes (ultra-straight or curled)?
   Ankles?
   Thighs and legs?
   Gluteal muscles?
   Arms?
   Shoulders?

Neck?

Chest?

Facial muscles?

Head/scalp?

If you were to look at yourself from the perspective of an outside observer, what muscular patterns might you notice? How might an observer see or describe you while in this state?

4. Next, let's change that belief around. Think of a time when you were completely free of this limiting belief. It's okay to use your imagination here.

If you're having difficulty thinking of a memory, make up a hypothetical one or think of someone who is free of that limiting belief and exemplifies the opposite.

5. Imagine emulating this new quality inside of yourself. Let this thought or memory magnify and permeate to every cell of your body to the point where you feel completely immersed in this newfound belief as if it's happening in the present time.

How do you hold yourself now? What are the physiological and muscular patterns you now observe?

In your mind's eye, see yourself from the outside looking in at yourself. How might an observer now see you? What's the difference?

6. Allow your muscles to soften, to melt. If your shoulders are raised, lower them. Close your eyes, as you examine any muscular tension you are still holding on to, and with your will and intention, release the holding in these regions.

Connect with your breath.
Pause.

7. Ask yourself: "What do I love the most about myself?"
Pause and wait for the answer.
And lastly, ask yourself: "How can I be just a little more loving to myself in this present moment?"

It doesn't matter how scared we are from the past or how long these self-limiting thoughts have been there. What matters is how you respond to each and every negative thought that arises in the moment…in this very moment. With practice, the process of witnessing our unconscious negative beliefs and changing them on the spot will become easier and easier.

Living in a world where we believe we are not good enough, or doing it wrong, or are deficient in any way is counter-productive for everyone. When we have a negative thought, it will attract more thoughts that find resonance with it. The same is true for positive thoughts. This is why we often find ourselves snowballing on upward or downward spirals. When one bad thing happens, it snowballs into other aspects of our life. And when we're on the "down," seeing the up feels like such a distant travel, but you are the one with your hand on the flashlight, and it is you who is choosing what to illuminate, and where your attention shines.

When on a downward spiral, having one simple positive thought is the first step toward excavating yourself out of the hole and getting yourself back on track. It can be as basic as "The sun feels great beating on my face" or "I love my little dog" or "I'm glad it's raining and filling the earth with water."

What's one positive thought that comes to your mind right now?

The above exercise is an abbreviated version of belief change work. For a more in-depth experience into altering your limiting beliefs and to learn how to stop your monkey mind of negative thinking and transform negative thoughts into positive ones, please see the belief change exercises in the accompanying workbook. Also, if you prefer to perform belief change work through audio or video, please see on my YouTube channel "How to Change a Belief" and "Healing the Wounded Inner-Child."

Integration

We were whole when we were born, and then life happened.

Perhaps you were made fun of one particular day at school and in that brief moment of torment, you detached from the part of yourself that felt joy and comfort in social situations. Or perhaps while still in your crib as a baby, you witnessed your parents fighting, and your spirit, out of fear, ran under the bed to hide. The part of you that felt safe and trust in the world around you vanished in that very moment.

During peak states of trauma, parts of our consciousness split. This process is known as fragmentation. Fragmentation most often occurs in our earliest years, when our brains and nervous systems are still forming, prior to the time when we are able to make conscious sense of the world around us. For a child, there is only so much fear and stress the body can handle before some aspect of it has to give.

You may be going through life until this very day trying to find and re-create these lost parts of yourself. However, such attempts will be unsuccessful until you learn how to meet each individual part's needs and reintegrate the parts back into the whole.

This "fragmentation" process occurs when, for instance, in the examples above, the part that felt joy and comfort in social situations split and was replaced by its shadow side—the aspect of you that feels insecure and inadequate in social situations. The part that felt like the world was safe and pristine with Mom and Dad split and was replaced by its shadow—the part of you that is afraid to trust others, as well as the world around you. Fragmentation occurs as a means of self-preservation.

To an observer, this may appear as if we have a momentary split personality, while on the inside, it feels more like an internal tug-of-war.

Close your eyes and ask yourself what parts of yourself do you feel you've rejected, ignored, or discarded?

Then, ask yourself who you would be if you were able to reclaim these lost parts and integrate them back into the whole. How might your life be different to this day?

For a more in-depth journey into reclaiming these lost parts of yourself and integrating them back into the whole, I encourage you to perform the Parts Integration exercise in the accompanying workbook.

"Find your true weakness and surrender to it. Therein lies the path to genius. Most people spend their lives using their strengths to overcome or cover up their weaknesses. Those few who use their strengths to incorporate their weaknesses, who don't divide themselves, those people are very rare. In any generation, there are a few and they lead their generation."
—***Moshe Feldenkrais***

Part IV

Diagnoses, Root Causes, and Perspectives for Healing

Before things come into reality, they come in as a thought form first. We form representative images in our mind of our thoughts all the time.

It's as simple as closing your eyes and imagining your favorite animal out in front of you, and voila, you will see a representative image of the actual thing; or craving a certain food such as a chocolate cake and you may see in your mind's eye the particular piece of cake with creamy frosting you so desire.

We will refer to the visual representation of the thought as a "picture." Some people see pictures more easily and vividly than others, yet this ability to see pictures can be expanded with practice. The clarity of your thoughts is often correlated to the clarity of the image you will see, and just the opposite is true as well, the clarity of your pictures can correlate to the clarity of your thoughts.

All pictures are influenced by our thoughts, memories, biases, and beliefs, and what we "see" in the outside world tells us a lot about what is going on in our subconscious.

The job of a clairvoyant or energy healer is to attempt to see pictures through their intuition centers, free of their prior biases, beliefs, and knowings, and secondly to interpret the meaning of what we see. Many healers also incorporate "clairaudience," (hearing the voices of others), and "clairsentience," (feeling the emotions of another), as well as other sensory modalities. We see, hear, feel and interpret information for our clients when, and only when, there is permission to do so.

Chapter 9:

Healing From the Root

In the Diagnoses/Ailments chart in the back of this book, I have outlined some of the thought patterns, "pictures," and beliefs I have found lie at the root of specific diseases and illness, as well as some healing suggestions. Use these suggestions (as outlined in the third column of the graph) loosely as a guide, for true healing will come when we heal the root cause (as outlined in the middle column) and create a whole different dynamic with this part of ourselves (for instance, the part that wants to be heard, to be acknowledged, or to be loved).

My intention with the healing suggestions is simply to point you in a certain direction for healing, and in no way do I mean to imply that through solely incorporating such suggestions, your long-standing chronic condition will suddenly resolve. Instead, these suggestions are holistic approaches that I might incorporate into my own practice and ones in which I have witnessed miraculous shifts occur when done right. As you read through the next section, rather than questioning how the "picture" and "beliefs" may or may not quite fit you, the way you will get the most out of this book is to hypothetically accept the information as true, and what's meant to stick will stick. Just like taking a multivitamin with a triple dose of all nutrients, your body will readily absorb what it needs, and the rest will be eliminated.

Perhaps it might even be helpful for you to phrase the "causes" of each diagnosis in column 2 of the graph, below, as follows: "If _____ were true, how then might that relate to me and my life?"

Go through the process of healing the issues as mapped out. Then, after you do so, if it worked and was helpful, keep it, and if not, move on. You have nothing to lose, right? After all, it's your pain we're talking about, and wouldn't you be willing to "try" any avenue that might help? And it's a free and natural approach.

The healing suggestions I listed, I purposely kept brief, and for many of them, vague. After all, the causality does indeed have some variance from person to person. And what works for one person most certainly might not work for the next. So, I give you full liberty to expand the interpretations as you see fit.

I encourage you to try a whole host of things to see what works best for you. If your therapist or friend taught you a technique that you find more effective for addressing the root cause, then use that one instead. My true intention with the suggestions is simply to point you in a certain direction. After all, identifying the root is a HUGE first step that can in and of itself evoke change.

Taking this concept one step further, let's say the diagnoses do present with a particular limiting belief, for instance, "I'm unworthy." This then presents a great opportunity to think back to the root of when this belief first began, back to your first few years of life, and ask yourself why that belief began for you in the first place. When you re-create the memory of this time, what you are seeing is a "picture" (even if you need to postulate or guess what was going on at this time).

Perhaps you had a father who was critical and an older brother who always acted like he was better than you. Whatever the situation, giving understanding and light as to the origin of such thought patterns is sometimes enough to alter your dynamic with it.

What you choose to do from here on out is up to you! (The workbook has further exercises & tools to work through stuck beliefs such as this one, and also see my belief change video on YouTube!)

Be patient and gentle with yourself as you work through the next section, as healing the underlying cause is not an easy task. Allow yourself to listen to your intuition and inner voice, as they will be the best guides to inform you as to where you may have fallen off course from your life's intended mission and what then needs to be done to bring yourself back.

Everything in our lives has a reason or "cause" for being there, which then produces an effect. Every belief we have stems from a "cause" at the level of our spirit body.

That is to say, there is something we are meant to learn and grow from with each limiting belief (and the dim circumstances that come with it). For instance, if someone believes they are unworthy, and hence get picked on at school, then their life's mission encompasses developing their self-worth! (More about this in chapter 12 as well as the last 2 chapters of the workbook.)

In the graph at the back of this book, the cause equates to our life lessons that must be learned (life's obstacles and hardships) and the effect is the outcome of learning such lessons (or not).

As you read the following section, I do expect a lot of doubt and defensiveness to arise. There was a time I would have reacted the same.

However, this is far from my intention. In fact, all I ask is for you to open your mind to the remote possibility that maybe, just maybe, there is some truth to it, and to stretch your mind just a little bit further than you may have done otherwise.

At this point in the book, I suggest you pause and refer to page 94 for further instructions on how to find the root cause plus healing perspectives for your ailments of past, present, and future.

Chapter 10:

Diagnoses Present Themselves as Themes

Shame lies at the root of impotence, difficulty having orgasms, infections, eating and digestive disorders, speech impediments, neck stiffness, and immune disorders, especially where the body attacks itself.

All throat-related issues, pneumonia, asthma, thrush, sore throat, a weak and timid voice, and so forth, have to do with personal power and communication, speaking one's truth, and feeling heard and understood.

All stomach pains and conditions have to do with self-sabotaging thoughts and behaviors, as well as holding on to other people's energy and emotions.

If one has chronic headaches, perhaps the lesson is around control (or fear of losing control) or micromanaging, trying so hard to understand/confusion, or one's unwillingness to look within for guidance. A separation from the head and the heart or body.

Frustration, angst, or "tumescent" (built up - PMS like energy) occurs when energy and emotions get backed up and stuck in our system. Over time, this "stuck" energy could contribute to a variety of medical conditions or injuries. After all, stubbing our toe or falling and breaking our ankle is one way to release this un-catalyzed energy from our systems when the energy gets to be too much, especially when our attempts to release the energy by healthy means are ineffective. Injuries and accidents are one way to release our pent-up energy and bring us back into our bodies.

Anxiety and worry have to do with a person fearing the future based upon past experiences. And more than likely they are mirroring a parent with this same tendency. This will always affect a person's breathing, causing tightness and constriction around their throat and chest region and result in diagnoses that have to do with blood flow, the heart, thyroid, or any issues around the major joints i.e., hips, shoulder, wrists as they habitually hold their extremities more tightly towards their core.

All feet and leg issues have to do with you walking forward on your path, as well as your connection to the current vibration of the planet.

All arm/hand issues have to do with blocks in the flow of your creative potential and in the physical act of "doing" that which you are meant to do or create out into the world.

All acne, rashes, fungi, herpes, and such types of skin disorders have to do with the body pushing away something in irritation, disgust, repulsion, and/or anger. Due to such long-standing emotions, the body is simply responding by rejecting some internal part of itself and pushing it out (onto the skin).

Sexual abuse trauma (especially from childhood) often presents itself in the internal organs that play some role in digestion such as the colon, the gut, the esophagus, the stomach, etc. Due to a feeling of disgust and repulsion, it is quite common for these people to have digestive issues or food allergies. When this person begins to uncover and heal such wounding, they may experience pain around the hip/buttock's region (such as sciatica) due to their tendency to over-contract these regions. The womb, heart, and sexual organs are other areas where the anger and pain may be somaticized.

Autoimmune disorders tend to occur when there is a childhood history of people (or a parent) or simply life itself, wanting more of them than they were able to give. In attempt to accommodate or please the family member(s) (and hence receive their love), they did give of themselves to the best of their abilities, yet later we will find, this came at a cost. (See page 59 and 105 for more details of this pattern.) It is a dichotomy that the natural coping mechanism that develops for this person is to hold back or protect how much of themselves they offer to others, while at the same they tend to have difficulty meeting their own needs. "I'm turning in on me."

If you want to know what your unresolved issues are, simply ask yourself what condition has already manifested in your body or what condition do you feel most prone to.

Sometimes these issues are generational—symptoms or traits passed on from previous generations—and then locked away in our unconscious (such as cancer). What is helpful to do in this case is to look at the specific memes, or emotional traits, that are patterns in your same-sex ancestors and realize what is yours and what is theirs.

Cancers are on the rise and there's a host of factors as to why, yet one of the many reasons, I believe, is due to the cumulative unhealed fear, worry and grief of previous generations that are still quite alive in us today.

This week, I did a reading on a woman named Martha. In her right hip, the doctors had diagnosed her cancer eight months ago. She'd gone through chemotherapy and numerous treatments, yet this lump still remained.

In my reading, I heard the words, "It's just a crutch."

"What is it a crutch for?" I asked her.

She replied, "Oh, my doubts that I can do it. I guess I need an extra leg to stand on."

She went on to explain how this is a period in her life where she has a lot of energy and wants to go do something to make a difference in the world, sort of like her last hurrah. "Time's a ticking," she stated, as she was in her late sixties. She had been feeling urgency and anxiety to do something about it, and she was constantly blaming her husband for things he was doing wrong.

I gathered more information from my reading on her that her entire life she'd been the one taking care of others, her two kids, who were now in their late- twenties, as well as her husband. And she now wished for more focus to be on herself.

As a young kid, she wasn't allowed to have the focus on herself. In fact, her mother punished her every time she did.

We continued with a series of a few more sessions focused on healing such unmet needs and limiting beliefs, and sure enough, the next time she went to see her Dr. and got retested, the cancer was untraceable.

My belief is that until we excavate, nourish, and begin to heal such specific emotions, thoughts, feelings, and segmented parts of ourselves, we are more likely to attract the associated diagnoses, as listed in the chart at the back of this book. Bacteria can be in a room filled with a hundred people, yet only the people with the vulnerability "pictures" that match will fall victim to attracting this bacterium their way.

Part V

Potentiating Your Life

In case you haven't guessed by now, the purpose of this book is actually to direct you along the path of your life purpose and to support you in clearing the roadblocks that stand in the way. And to help you to access the healing powers that are quite alive within you!

It's certainly no mistake that throughout all the generations of evolutionary history, the planet or Source has waited until now to bring you into existence and has created your eyes, your ears, your hair color, your shape, your ethnicity, and all the other unique qualities of you, to be the person you are today. We may think it is random selection, but can we be open to the possibility that there may be an even grander plan in store for us.

Chapter 11:

Your Soul's Journey

We entered this world as a pure innocent child with a clean slate. From day one, the people and experiences around us began influencing our internal landscape.

Every cell of our body aligned according to our self-concept (like the master control of a data processor), thus affecting our motor and coordination patterns, as well as our physiological states.

The beliefs we had as a young child all became ingrained in our bodies at a cellular level so much so that they eventually produced circumstantial evidence, which then further supported our self-negating beliefs, further supporting the very person we are today and the experiences we attract around us.

The consistency of this predicament is almost humorous. We could have years of psychotherapy to resolve the circumstances in our lives of being partner-less or broken in one way or another, yet in order to truly heal an issue, it MUST be healed at a deep cellular level.

"What was it I did or said that had him feel like I was too much?" you might ask. For most, it's merely unobservable to the untrained human eye.

The fact that the same patterns exist time and time again is enough to prove to you that it is still there. When the world reacts to us in a different way (over a period of time), then that is the strongest indicator that a neurological shift has taken place, and that change has occurred within-side us at a cellular level.

Everyone in human existence responds to these subconscious messages of another. It's one of the biggest secrets known to humankind. We think we can hide certain aspects of who we are (many of us attempt this behind the walls of our chest and ribcage). Or we may think thoughts that we believe others are unable to feel or hear (as if they were private).

We try to hide the fact that we believe others are better than us, that we feel worthless at times, that we've made shameful mistakes, and that we've lived a very small existence. Even though these traits may not be outwardly visible to others, the neuropeptides in another's subconscious still respond.

This subconscious communication system can be termed "meta-messages," messages that exist beyond actual verbal communication, behind what we can see, feel, or hear. Metamessages influence the lens through which we view others as well as the way we may feel when in another's presence.

You may be wondering, why some people attract certain people to themselves while other people seem to repel them? Why do some people find themselves constantly in relationships while others are always single? Why do repeated health mishaps and injuries happen to some yet not to others? Why does abundance and success find some while others who work just as hard remain broke? Why do certain people always find themselves at the brunt of the blame? And why does person-A have a particular dynamic with person-B, yet person-C has a completely different interaction with person-A?

It is because we all have a unique feeling signature that communicates subconsciously (through meta-messages) with one another in accordance with every aspect of who we are. It is sort of like when women spend a good deal of time together and their menstruation cycles become in sync or when two lovers live together and their taste buds and breathing rates begin to harmonize. They may even begin to speak and look alike over time. Whether we like it or not, just our mere presence evokes a world of information about who we are to another being.

What we're talking about here is a vibrational energy that exists in every moment of our lives. Everything in the universe is now understood to be made out of energy; to our perception, it appears physical and solid, yet in reality, it is all energy, and energies interact. When you interact in your environment, you are both absorbing and sending out energy at the same time. Every atom of your body absorbs and emits energy continuously.

If you rushed into a room in a panic because you were running late, or you just witnessed a fight, the entire ecosystem around you will respond accordingly. People will adjust their breathing rates, the position of their shoulders, and the openness of their eyelids accordingly. All living organisms communicate with these vibrations.

As the stem cell biologist, Bruce Lipton, states, "When we are not paying attention to our vibrational energies, we are missing the most important readouts from our environment." He goes on to say, from understanding the new physics, we learn that all energies are entangled and interact with each other. Therefore, you need to pay attention to these invisible forces that are going on all around you. And one of the best ways to do this is to tune into yourself!

The key point here is that if we want the circumstances in the outside world to change, we need to change the part of ourselves that is the "attractor" to what is. This is the crux of the work I do with individuals and the reason why my clients have such significant success in altering long-held patterns. My focus is on altering the aspect of the client (be it their thoughts, beliefs, and/or cellular memories of the past) with the realities of who they are today and the direction of their intended destiny.

For instance, if a client is feeling tension, worry, or fear toward a superior at work, we may work together to convert such feelings to understanding, empathy, and ease. And then I may help her to reclaim a sense of empowerment. We may end the session by creating a new contract or energetic agreement between the two of them, one that feels workable and in alignment for both parties.

As a result of such work, the dynamic between the two of them has to shift. I often get asked by clients if the other person is having the experience we are working on along with us, and my belief is yes (at a subconscious cellular level, of course).

Seeing and understanding what is going on at a cellular level of a person (even a stranger) doesn't require clairaudience or psychic abilities, for surely, I cannot possibly claim to know the inner workings of your being any better than you. Moreover, it requires us to tune in deeper to how we are feeling to receive the sentient messages from another person and to note the impacts we are having on the world around us.

Chapter 12:

A Journey in Search of Our Life's Purpose

What if the major negative life themes and lessons were all intelligently crafted to teach you the lessons you needed to learn to walk your life's highest path?

Let's just for imagination's sake say that a higher being has intellectually crafted all of the life experiences that have come before you for a grander purpose, all to create the person and the life you are living today. All those hardships, losses, and states of suffering lead to "the now." They are all aligning with your soul's journey to help teach you the lessons you need to learn in this very lifetime.

Let's just hypothesize for a mere few minutes that we choose everything we have in our lives today. We may easily (or not so easily) see how we choose our car, our career, our house, and the clothes we wear on our back today. Yet let's just push our imagination button a little bit further and say we choose the friends we have, the people who stop us on the street, the hardships we face in life, and the conflicts that arise in our personal relationships. Let's even venture to make the far-off assumption that we choose our mother and father and all our family members (just as they too choose you). You might be thinking, how could this possibly be so? I had nothing to do with my mother and father before I came into inception. The job I hate found me. And the car accident that occurred last week was certainly not of my choosing.

You might be thinking:

If this is so, why don't my parents love me?

If this is so, why did he physically abuse me?

If this is so, why do I feel as if there's nothing to live for?

If this is so, why do I have to endure this pain and illness?

You do have a perfectly justifiable reason to be angry, resentful, jealous, and overwhelmed with the circumstances of your life. You may want to curse and scream and lash out with anger. After all, we've been taught our entire life that the world exists outside of us and it is a mere circumstance that it happened as it did. We'll go to great lengths to figure out why "it" is happening to us.

You may say, "I do meditation, I feel gratitude, and I do all I can to live a life of love and happiness, how possibly can this concept then be so?" You might even say, "My life was perfect, and everything was going just fine before this injury occurred."

Yet hidden deep below, in that space where only keen observers can see, there are little twinges of self-inflicted invalidation and perfectionist ideals, or some thought processes that are a "match" to the manifestation of what is. The truth is we are unaware of how powerful we are in the deep interplay of our beliefs, thoughts, and/or actions, and the role they play in dictating all the events and circumstances in our lives. We are causing a deep injustice to humankind to play small enough to believe that these things are outside of our control.

Pain as Opportunity

What if, taking the perspective, that every ache, pain, or malalignment on the physical and mental planes, is actually an opportunity, an opportunity to achieve new heights in your evolution, to heal your deepest and most wounded parts of yourself, the parts that you may have decided (consciously or not) to discard and forget, and, instead, to learn to begin to love or find peace and acceptance in these areas? And, with introspection and healing, to bring yourself back to balance, back into reunion with the desired course of the soul?

Belief is everything here. If your thoughts align with wellness, opportunity, and healing, and you truly connect with the concept of how powerful you are in affecting everything that occurs in, on, and around you, you will prove yourself right. If you believe a cure is hopeless and you won't get better, you're right again.

The law of attraction states that like attracts like. That means that when you have a thought, it will attract more thoughts that find resonance with the first. This is why we often find ourselves snowballing on upward or downward spirals. When one bad thing happens, it snowballs into other aspects of our lives. And when we're on the "down," seeing the up feels like such a distant travel.

When this occurs, having one simple positive thought is the first step toward excavating yourself out of the hole and getting yourself back on track. It can be just as basic as "the sun feels great beating on my face," "I love my little dog," or "I'm glad it's raining and watering my grass or garden."

What is one positive thought that comes to your mind right now as you read this?

Any illness you have and any negative experience you have is a direct experience of the fact that you haven't fully loved yourself. You have not fully followed what you truly wish to do.

How is it that we have not hearkened to the voice of our soul?

What is it that your inner guidance system wants you to hear?

Chapter 13:

Lifting the Veil

Since you have journeyed with me to this point, I want to commend you for the wonderful job you have done of lifting the veil of what lies beneath the pain. Yet it is now critical that you replace what lies underneath with that which is much more replenishing and healing.

Our souls want to laugh. Our souls want to dance. Our souls want to inspire and help others. Our souls crave connection and to know our greatest purpose.

You have been given the opportunity to make a unique and individual contribution to this planet and to humanity. And perhaps, in some unconscious way, your reason for picking up this book may have been to find it. Inherently, we don't want to sit on the couch day after day and let life pass us by.

We want to live it! We want life to use us in the way in which we were truly meant to be used, where our light is able to magnify and radiate the strongest.

When we start to use ourselves in this way, we reciprocally become sourced in a complementary fashion with more power, more light, and more fuel, and in such an interplay, we all win.

When we truly are in flow with the ebb and flow of our abilities and gifts, this will holographically spread throughout our body, affecting things such as our muscular coordination, our balance, our health, and our longevity. As your internal landscape changes, it impacts all areas of your life.

You become less worried about what others think of you and more focused on the impact you are making in the collective consciousness of the whole. You do things less out of obligation and responsibility and more out of sheer will and desire.

When you are in the flow, you will have more energy and more enthusiasm. You will smile more, laugh more, and you will see more. You'll feel good about how you use your time. You'll amaze yourself by sleeping deeper and more peacefully yet requiring much fewer hours of sleep. Your body will feel more ignited and turned on. You'll attract higher vibrational opportunities and people your way. And your capacity to love and see the good in people will expand.

We are all on a mission to find our "joie de vivre" ("joy of life") and you are cheating all of us here on this planet by not fully potentiating and sharing it for the greater good.

The goal of going through the healing process is to retrace our steps, to revisit needs that weren't fulfilled, to acknowledge those needs no matter how painful that process, and to find a way to fill them now. Wherever and whenever our creative process stopped, this is where we abandoned parts of ourselves and allowed our subconscious to then fragment.

It is now that we are choosing to reconnect with these lost parts and become whole once again.

Our Individuated Purpose

Each of our souls enters our bodies, bringing with it a unique and individuated purpose and perspective. As we enter our late thirties and forties or perhaps even fifties, many of us may find we are spending a good deal of our lives searching for it. We may find ourselves working at a job that is unfulfilling or having a relationship where our basic needs are not being met. We may be aware of our gifts and talents, some of which we've learned with proficiency, but still knowing that we are slightly off the mark of finding our true bliss. Many of us spend years, even a good majority of our adult lives, searching for such direction.

Each one of us was incarnated here on earth with a particular mission. In order to head in the direction of our soul's path, we have been taught life lessons that are in a sense the polarity to our life's greatest hardships, for it is these particular topics that our souls have chosen as the focus of areas to research and improve upon.

These lessons may include healing suppressed anger, finding the strength to rise up against the oppression of men, feeling that we matter, feeling "worthy," and feeling beautiful. Once we learn each individual lesson, then they no longer remain a cog in the wheel of our life, and we can synchronistically stop attracting the circumstances and situations that are a match to them. And, even better, these learned lessons are the very things that will propel you full throttle toward your intended destiny. What might that be? What is your higher calling?

Perhaps your purpose is to help others to reclaim their voice and feel beautiful on the inside. Perhaps you are meant to be an advocate for animal rights and feel guided to open an animal foster home. Or perhaps you are a human rights activist for topics such as girls who are entrapped into sexual slavery, and it was your experience of growing up in an abusive home and being mistreated and disregarded by your father that fueled the fire that now burns viciously inside of you around these issues. And your peace of mind will only be found once you take action.

Take a moment now and reflect, if my life's greatest hurdles and struggles were healed, who then would I be? What might I be doing? How might it feel inside?

Sometimes life lessons come in small packages like the frustration we experience after running late and missing the bus once again or dealing with the children's screaming voices. At other times, they're more penetrating such as being fired from a job, experiencing chronic pain throughout our body, living a life of feeling on the outside, being abused, or constantly finding ourselves the target of blame.

Maybe you needed to learn autonomy. Maybe you needed to learn how to stand up for yourself and not to always be the one who either gets victimized or holds most of the responsibility in the relationship. Maybe you needed to learn to soften your controlling side. However, the lessons are delivered, when we are able to extract the wisdom and learning from our past hardships, this furthers our progression. When we harbor anger and resentment of these lessons, this hinders our progression.

I encourage you to continue this path of inquiry to further examine the core lessons, struggles, and themes of your life and how they might indirectly relate to your life purpose. (For further instructions on how to do this, please see the Finding Your Blissful Calling exercise in the accompanying workbook.)

Have Faith

It's understandable that when in the midst of a disease, injury, heartbreak, or an abusive relationship, you may be unable to see the light at the end of the tunnel. The pain and hurt may run so deep that all you want is for the hurting to stop. Staying alive in the whirl of it may be as much as you can handle. Hence, if you have found symptom-relieving strategies that work for you, I am a proponent for you using them to find a respite from suffering. When we are free of significant pain, it's much easier to then place our attention on our feeling body, our pleasures, and our desires.

Your search for recovery and peace of mind can get exhausting. Have faith. There is something greater in store for you in this lifetime. Life has created such a custom-made and complex labyrinth for you so that you can find yourself.

You have come to earth at this time on assignment, to make a shift and assist in the transition toward higher consciousness. It is my hope that this book will be just one of many tools assisting you in bringing your own knowledge forward.

You are needed. You've been training for this assignment for lifetimes.

I'm going to leave you with just a few closing remarks.

The first, being the good or not such good news, is that this journey never ends. It continues from the day we are born until the day we die. And then it starts once again all over again. The best we can do is to learn to enjoy this journey, however complicated or painful it is. Remember, the lens through which we view it then determines what we see.

There will come a day when you are sitting on your deathbed (if not before) when you will turn and look back at it all and sigh. And in that last gasp of breath, all will be forgiven, all will be forgotten, all will be forsaken, and we will be no more.

Healing from the Root (Instructions)

How to Use the Diagnoses/Ailments Chart

Step 1: Make a list of all your ailments and diagnoses and see if you can find your diagnoses or ailment(s) listed in the following chart.

Step 2: Come to a space of quiet contemplation. Close your eyes and bring your focus toward the center of your head. Allow your face, eyes, and entire body to soften. Take a few deep inhales and exhales as you allow yourself to clear your mind.

Step 3: Visualize the "picture," words or beliefs, associated with each diagnosis (as written in the center column of the graph). Ask yourself how this may metaphorically or literally apply to your life.

Step 4: Perform any and all healing suggestions that seem to fit. For some of the ailments, I refrained from writing a healing suggestion. If this is the case, use your intuition here. What might be needed to resolve the root cause? Allow yourself a few moments of inner reflection and contemplation time.

Diagnoses/Ailments Chart

Disease/ Problem	Root	Perspectives for Healing
Abdominal Pain (See Also "Menstrual Cramps.")	A block in the flow of vital energy. Feeling inept "I made a mistake." Shame, "I need to hide to feel safe." "I'm unworthy." "I deserve this." Can also be related to childbirth-related issues or femininity.	Solution = self-love Affirmations: "I am enough." "I am free to take up space." "I belong." "I deserve."
Acne	Discontent, stress, angst, social pressures, irritation, frustration, lack of self-acceptance, invalidation, and judgment A "heating up" from the inside. "Get out of here!" A shield of protection to help push intimacy away. Back acne, pushing the past behind you.	Reclaim a sense of identity and self-worth separate from those around you (so you no longer feel the need to push others away). Find what you are good at (for instance, playing an instrument or sport) and nurture that! Focus upon what is special and unique about you. Come into full acceptance of the moment, as opposed to wanting to be somewhere else. Catch your monkey mind of thoughts when you feel it wandering off, in judgments, comparisons, and negative thinking. Perform belief change and parts integration work (See workbook).

| ADD (Attention Deficit Disorder) | The strong pull of spirit to leave the consciousness and confines of the body.

They may have a tendency to feel more restricted in authoritative and controlled environments, where they "should" be a certain way, as this conflicts with their true spirit and will give them less reason to be "here" and more reason to be "there."

"I'm invisible." "Something is wrong with me." "I'm on the outside." "I don't belong here."

Judgment, personal power issues, invalidation, comparison

With hyperactive ADD, the spirit gets stuck inside the confines of the body, bombarding up against the inside edges in its continual attempts to leave. This can create agitation. "Wee, this is fun!" | The primary question to ask here is:
• WHY does this person want to continuously leave his/her body?
• What does being present and in the body mean to him/her and why might this person view it as a threat?
• What might this person fear to feel?
• What are some ways you can help your inner child to feel safer in such a situation?

Grounding exercises (See page 179): Nature is great for you!

Body/being (See the workbook.)

Surround yourself with people who can see your unique qualities and gifts and who don't try to put you in "the box" or tell you how you "should" be.

Personalized attention or small groups are ideal for learning. |
|---|---|---|

Allergies	"Yikes!" Resistance Food allergies – "I can't stomach that."	Think back to when you last had your allergy attack. Then ask yourself how this experience felt inside of your body. Is there something that triggers your allergic reaction? See if you can find some correlation between the thing you are allergic to and potentially the first time you may have experienced a similar state of contraction in your body. Ask yourself: • "When was the first time you ever experienced this feeling state?" • What were you resisting at this time? • How and why might these negative associations have formed (even if the correlation to when you first felt this way and what you are allergic to doesn't make sense). The key is to find the root cause of an allergy and then begin to form positive associations with it. I.E., with 1 client who developed food allergies right after the time she was sexually abused, we realized the foods she developed reactions to were the same foods her abuser would have eaten. Often with allergies, it's not so straightforward. For instance, you might be allergic to dirt or pollen. Yet, in actuality, there can be some toxin or chemical in the dirt or pollen that is giving you the reaction, rather than the pollen itself. If this is the case, your allergic reaction is simply a mechanism created to push away the toxin in order to maintain a state of balance and greater homeostasis. Thanking your body in this regard is one step in the right direction. Create a safety barrier around you to keep out toxins and chemicals so you can feel safe and trust the world around you (See "Boundaries" in the workbook).

Aids (See "HIV.")		
Alopecia (for females)	"Get out of my hair!"	Forgiveness of those who have hurt you, particularly Mother and female ancestry.

Any technique you can find to transmute irritation, anger, and resentment into understanding, love, and compassion.

Cutting Cords and Emotional Body exercises (See the workbook). |
| Anemia | Picture-sparsely populated red cells floating slowly and without directionality through thick fluid, lacking connection with the other cells.

"I'm lost."
"I'm alone."
"I don't really have what it takes to make it."

Fear of life. | Find a solid support system that validates you.

Find activities you enjoy doing that connect you back into your body such as Feldenkrais, spending time in nature, hiking, etc., and cultivate that which inspires you and gives you a sense of purpose. |

Ankle/Foot, Swollen Ankle	Picture #1, a chain around your ankle, which is attached to someone or something from the past, preventing you from moving forward Picture #2, slamming on the breaks of your car, yet your foot can't quite find the break. Picture #3, child fearing punishment from a caregiver, and bracing yourself from his/her wrath. Hopelessness and fears around moving forward. Doubt and powerlessness.	Cording exercises (See workbook.) Use either the car or the chain analogy (whichever image you most resonate with) as a metaphor and ask yourself what it might represent in your current life. • Might it be time passing by and you feel powerless to stop it or might it be the feeling of someone or something holding you back? • Make a list of your beliefs that are behind this. Then decide what you want instead of this. • Make a list of the "next steps" to take in order to walk in the direction of what you truly want. Commit to taking at least the first steps this week if possible. Have an accountability buddy, friend, coach, or spouse support you. Walking your path and Belief change exercises (See the workbook.)

Ankle Sprain	Cross motives where you may say one thing while thinking and feeling another "I'm turning in on myself." Feeling compromised around purpose/career-type issues.	Feldenkrais lessons focused on foot/leg/ankle. Journal about the aspects of your life you feel compromised around. Ask yourself: • "If I didn't compromise myself here, what might that look like?" • "What is it I'm being dishonest with myself and others around?" • "If I was to tell the truth here, what might that look like?" Walking path exercise (See the workbook.)

Anorexia (See Also "Digestion or ADD if appropriate.")	Picture-hiding oneself in the sliver of the doorway, which represents the zone between the physical plane and the spirit world. A strong pull to leave the earthly plane, to leave the uncomfortable confines of the body. Self-hate, shame, guilt, and a perilous depriving of oneself of one's needs. Feeling controlled and powerless Feeling isolated and alone "I don't deserve to be here." A desire to hide and become invisible Pressure to perform better	Heal the wounds that the addiction is simply covering up, specifically around the feelings of shame, invalidation, and unworthiness. Learning self-love is the most crucial element to healing this. Family therapy can be helpful, as ALL eating disorders are family disorders. No parent or guardian is benign in the development of a person feeling this way about him- or herself. Find people who are capable of loving you for who you truly are. This is easier said than done, as anorexia is also an isolation disorder where the person will lock their internal doors and be resistant to letting anyone come in. • Preplanned scheduled meals (although they may initially resist this idea). Belief change/inner-child healing and the Body-Image exercise in workbook. If you are a parent to someone struggling with this disorder, ask yourself: • Are there any behaviors or circumstances you are aware of (from yourself or others) which might be contributing to their feelings of disempowerment or not mattering? • How emotionally connected are you to your child and what if anything can you do to have your child feel safe in sharing with you? Recognize (depending on your child's severity) most likely they have few or no friends, no one to turn to for support and love. The pain and hurt they are feeling may result in them wanting to push you away as well. Continue to provide them empathy and love regardless of their actions and behavior.

Anxiety	"Oh no, I gotta get it done. I gotta get it done right." "I can't do anything right."	When faced with anxiety, your energy will instantly go to your chest and head (sixth/seventh chakra), hence, reconnect with your feet, the earth, the physical space around you (page 179).
	The root is one of two things or most likely a combination: 1. As a child, doing your best to appease your mom's (or caregiver's) needs or what was "needed" of you in the household. 2. Taking on the worries and anxieties from your mother or caregiver through mirroring and matching their feelings and behaviors. Running your energy in future time, circling of thoughts, fears, and worries of what's to come, disconnection from your physical body, and/or feeling lost and isolated in your experience.	Practice being in the now, focusing completely on this moment, and this moment only. Share your thoughts and fears either in writing or with a confidant so you don't have to keep all the worries circling in your head. Whatever it takes to release worry, fear, and guilt. Find activities to diffuse the buildup of energy such as laughing, dancing, music, and aerobic exercise. Breathing and relaxation techniques. Take a deep breath and know this too shall pass. Allow yourself to be held—big bear hugs can help you to let go of some of the excess energy you're holding on to. At times it may be appropriate to push through this feeling and have the brevity to step into what you are truly passionate about. You may have a subconscious addiction to this feeling of "being on the edge" and your higher calling maybe just on the other side. Live your bliss! Avoid sugar, caffeine, high-glycemic foods, fried foods, and caffeine. Body/being and belief change work. (See the workbook).

Arthritis (Rheumatoid)	Self-criticism Fatigue from holding generational wounding for so long. "I'm tired of this." "I need to get things done." "I can do better."	Go easy on yourself. Self-love/less critical Feldenkrais hand/finger lesson (See my YouTube channel.) Family constellation/family systems work/ancestral healing
Arthritis (Osteo.)	Pushing forward in life Left side: Self-protection, defense of identity Right side: Halting/freezing	(See Hip and Leg suggestions, as appropriate.)
Asperger's	"I need to stay in 'here' (the labyrinth of the mind). "I can't go out and play, despite the fact that I want to."	

Asthma	Powerlessness, difficulty breathing in life, feeling stifled or even trapped. They're coming to get me, urgency to take action fast.	What in your life right now are the stressor(s) that may be contributing to your difficulty breathing and tightness around your chest and throat? What would it take to help you to breathe in life more and cultivate a feeling in your chest of spaciousness and ease? Consider getting a vaporizer, diffuser, or anything that will help you to fill your lungs with fresh air. Affirmation – I breathe in the freshness of life.
Autism	No one is home. Unavailable for the superficiality of life. Preference to be elsewhere. Only 2 percent needs to be here (and BTW, that 2 percent can be enough to handle Einstein-like equations).	Life (in the physical form) matters!

Autoimmune Disorders Such as SIBO (Small Intestine Bacterial Overgrowth)	Picture-a little girl reaching up for her mother's arms, wanting to be seen, loved, and held, yet her mother is unable to truly see her. "I'm unlovable." Feeling unsupported Always taking care of others, which results in me running on empty. "Nobody is appreciating me. I'm being taken for granted." Others sucking your nutrients out of you. "My life has been pulled out of me."	If you're in a partnership with someone, figure out what emotional nutrients both of you are deficient in. Have a conversation about how you can best meet each other's emotional needs, (especially in order to prevent relationships from feeling exhausting.) Wounded inner-child and belief change exercise—whatever it takes for you to feel more nourished, seen, and supported in the way you most need and want. See also Boundaries exercise in Workbook.
Balding	Cerebral: Lacking connection with spirit and "Source." Picture-a huge gap between the crown of your head and the spirit-world above. Both have a desire to connect with each other, yet there's simply an empty space in between blocking the communication. Spirits supportively laugh and say, "You didn't have to lose your hair to get closer to us."	Connect with a higher power, faith, universal energy, in whatever way feels suitable for you. This might also require you to take a momentary break from your "heady" career or that which causes you stress to reclaim this aspect of yourself. Some of the numerous ways to do this include the following: • Solo walks in the woods • Deep-breathing exercises • Attending a service of your religious or spiritual preference • Volunteering at a shelter • Meditation • Sound healing/reiki

Back Pain by Region (from Upper to Lower Back)		
Back/Upper Trapezius (Shoulder) Region (See also Neck/Shoulder)	Hiding, shame, guilt, lacking emotional support, effort, blocking love, self-protection, pressure to do more. "It's all my fault."	Find some way to receive the love and support you need. Affirmation – "I am supported." Belief Change/Inner Child Healing (See the workbook). Anything it will take to help you to restore your confidence and seniority so you can open your heart (chest) and radiate your true light forward.
Back Mid to Shoulder-Blade Region	Mental drive to get somewhere fast & accomplish your goals yet burdened with a busy mind and the stressors of life. (Often with head positioned in front of spine). Fear of getting left behind. "I got to take more upon myself." "It's all up to me."	Develop both your tactfulness and your ability to ask for support from others. Soften your eyes and widen your perspective and vision. Think about what you're holding on to (responsibility and guilt-wise). Imagine taking this off your back and bringing it out in front of you. See if you can look at it from a new perspective. How do you wish to relate to this person or thing? For instance, can you be more playful with it, designate responsibility, etc.? Ideally, you want to ease the burden this thing is causing you and come to a place of more acceptance and spaciousness inside. Cutting cords and belief change exercises (See the workbook.) Feldenkrais – I.E. Foam roller lined up with spine series (*A Quick Guide to Easing Pain/* also in my *Comfort for Life DVD*), or the exercise suggested below for low back pain.
Back - Hunchback	Responsibility, burdens, and anything you don't want to look at, throw it onto your back. "Get off my back!"	

Back Pain, Lower	Carrying the weight of the world. Obligation and resented responsibility. The emotional burden of life. Life's hardships and responsibilities weighing on you. Responsibility/ Effort Backing out of that which your soul truly wants. A difficulty looking at the past.	As stated above, anything that is behind, we must bring to the forefront. We must alter our relationship with effort, obligation, and responsibility. We must heal our old karmic patterns and familial imprinting, release ourselves from the burdens and guilt we've been holding on to, and reclaim a sense of freedom and choice from inside ourselves. Cutting cords, emotional release, and belief change exercises (See the workbook). Hip opener yoga and exercises and Feldenkrais series...i.e., roll up a washcloth and while lying on your back on a yoga mat or carpet, place it parallel to your ribs yet in the region where you have pain. Then do small, gentle, pelvic tilts. Avoid halting your breath. Allow your breath and the movement to be rhythmic. Make sure it's a pelvic roll and not a lift! Do 10-15 repetitions, then remove the washcloth, remain on your back, and feel if there's any improvement. If so, do another set with the washcloth placed in a slightly different region.
Back – Herniated Disc	We're going this way - stubbornness to yield. Fierce determination, with suppressed or held in emotions. Cross Motivations	Widen your perspective to see if perhaps there's anything in life you are forcing your way through. Ice the region with a cold pack the first couple of days post-injury. Feldenkrais is wonderful for this! Most likely you have been walking through life like you're wearing a strait jacket. Reteach your body how to move segmentally and with more freedom.

Birth Defects	Karmic, unfinished business	Karmic and ancestral healing.
Bladder - (Inability to Empty Bladder Fully)/Urinary Incontinence	"I'm afraid to come out."	Anything it will take to release such contraction, holding, and fear.
Bloated Belly/Flatulence (See Also "Constipation.")	Picture-gas bubbles pushing up against the inner walls representing old stuck and stagnant emotion pushing to get out. Isolation Feelings of irritation and powerlessness. Feeling "pushed out," yet emotionally, "holding it in." In women over the age of 40, the "bloat" can also be associated with the void of pregnancy (or possibly as a result of pregnancy).	Avoid eating late at night, for this could hinder the processing of emotions that occurs in our dreams (as our internal body functions are directed toward digestion rather than resting). Find some way to express the emotions that wish to be acknowledged and heard. When you are living your bliss and truthful calling, your energy won't stagnate. So, your task is to find it! (See the Blissful Calling exercise in the workbook.) (See also "Constipation," below.)

| Breasts | Represents nurturing and nourishment and giving energy to others. |
| | Cysts, cancers, etc., form when we either over-nurture others or under-nurture ourselves. |

Bulimia	Picture-purging self-hatred: "I can't hold it all in; I must release it." Holding in the responsibility, emotions, and stuff of others. Feelings of shame, inadequacy, unworthiness, and insignificance. Eating disorders come about in an environment where there is a strong moral code of that which is right versus wrong, so there is pressure to get everything right. However, you'll never get everything right, which then may likely confirm your self-limiting beliefs that you are not enough, or something is wrong with you. The pattern works like this. Because I am not doing it right, this means I am "bad" and deserving of punishment. Hence, I must punish myself by sadomasochistic or self-flagellating behavior. Then, after I give myself proper punishment, this means I'm "good," and I want to be good. Also, over time, the physical feeling of being full will be linked to the judgment of being fat which is linked to the feeling of being bad and unlovable, hence, continues this feedback loop. Following the purging, "feel-good" hormones are released, which then eases their self-imposed pressures and feelings of inadequacy and gives them a momentary feeling of pleasure and relief (hence further reinforcing this pattern). Also, after the release, they reconnect with their sincere feeling of deservingness. "I DO deserve to feel good about myself," (even though they arguably spent a good deal of their lives convincing themselves otherwise).

Cancer (Esophageal)	Picture-a large, animated throat canal that the voice can't get through. Hence, the lips are moving, yet there's no voice coming out. Angst, frustration, irritation, unexpressed anger, suppressed communication	Healing revolves around your true voice and expression coming out. If you have difficulty expressing yourself in words, especially if the person you want to say the words to is unavailable to hear them (or deceased), or if stating them directly may be inappropriate or offensive, here are some suggestions: • Journal or write a letter. Write out everything you truly want to say yet haven't been able to. If you want, you can read what you wrote to a neutral person. Or you can burn the paper, toss it into the sea, or do any ritual that helps with completion. • Have someone guide you on a cathartic release, where they might have you punch a pillow, etc. while speaking what it is you have held back on saying. • Perform the Emotional Release exercises in the workbook. Get more in touch with your body. The important thing for you is to first get in touch with your internal world and secondly to share such experiences with another. One way is to describe sensations in as much detail as possible. Find a neutral willing person to participate in this exercise with you. You can have them ever so slightly touch your arm and go into as much detail as possible with the sensations you are feeling. Practice describing your internal experience in detail without using any charge or judgment. Withhold & De-cording exercises (See the workbook).

Cancer (Ovarian)	Picture-your right ankle chained in shackles. "I'm trapped." "I can't get out." Lack of resolution around children (or lack of). Sexual abuse at an early age or neglect, disappointment in intimate relationships, or a lack of intimacy.	
Cancer (Throat/Lymph)	"My voice doesn't matter." Stiffness and rigidity around the chest/throat area in an attempt to be a certain way (which others expect you to be).	(See "Chest," "Throat," or "Cancer (Esophageal)" suggestions.)
Carpal Tunnel	Picture-pushing a box up a mountain with wrists extended. Push, push, push— "I'm always being pushed to do more." "Stop doing that to me." "Life is so hard." "Finally, a place I can rest." Angst, frustration, type-A behavior	

Cerebellar Issues/Balance (See Also "Vertigo.")	Picture-person walking through a white room where all the walls, floor, and ceiling are moving in and out, like a horror film. Feeling unsafe and unsupported: "I'm all alone." "I'm trapped." "Get me out of here." Themes of codependency versus isolation These people will put a lot of pressure on themselves to handle and make sense of the world around them. The root of such issues stems from childhood when as an infant, there was enough chaos and instability in the world around you to have you feel unsafe and unsupported at times. The only choice you had in such a situation was to "match" the chaos or confusion going on most likely inside of your mother in order to receive her love. You also felt the need to remain on high alert to figure out how to best handle the world around you. "Are we turning right?" "No left." "Is she okay?" "What should I do?" As a young infant, you were already taking the driver's seat prior to your brain being developed enough to logically know what to do, resulting in a great deal of effort and stress, and pressure in your chest, throat, and head. Now, as an adult, your challenge may be to find the calm in the storm and live a life that feels safe and spacious.

Chest Tightness	Picture-the ribs forming the jail cell that we lock ourselves into. Attempting to break free of the past, confusing the jail cell with a means of self-protection. The right-chest region hardens to block the blows of life.	In meditation, journey to the time when the metaphorical "jail cell" was first created for you. • What was it protecting you from? • Who did you want to keep out? • What did you fear in the outside world at that time? Judgment, other people's perspectives, etc.? • How might the jail cell have served you at that time? • How is it serving you now? • What is it currently protecting you from? Although it may have been true that you needed to protect yourself in this way during your youngest years, ask yourself if it's true that you still need to protect yourself from whatever it is you fear. • If the answer is "No," ask your higher self what it will take to dissolve the jail cell. • If the answer is "Yes," what do you want that protection to look like? How do you want to feel when you are around whatever it is you fear? Commit to that. Soften your heart and find some way to use compassion in what you do. Belief change/inner-child work

Chronic Fatigue	This pattern begins with extreme hyper-vigilance with the need to be on full alert, followed by: "The world is turning in on me," "I can't cope." "I can't carry it all." It is at this point that the symptoms set in. The muscles throughout the body have become so habitualized to work on overdrive that they have lost their innate capacity to "let go" and rest. The need to be heard and understood. The need to be a "good" person. The need to be responsible and fulfill obligations. Fearing the future, unable to accept the now. There is also a tendency to absorb other people's and Spirit's energies into your personal space.	Grounding—Feel your two feet on the ground and connected to the earth. Bring your energy from your mind down into your feet (See page 179). Cutting cords exercise—Release responsibility and other people's energy (See the Workbook). Stop "doing." Stop all the effort and mental chatter that is going on inside of you. Learn to surrender control and to stop beating yourself up for being less than who or where you believe you "should" be. See if you can perform daily tasks with less muscular awareness. Feldenkrais will help you to let go of this excess muscular tension that you might be subconsciously holding on to. (See suggestions for "Fibromyalgia.")

Cold (Head Cold/Sore Throat)	Simply the body's way of trying to catch up with itself—the "being" has moved way in front of the "body" and the being is having difficulty keeping up. This can be due to either fear or excitement of what is to come (control). Most likely, we have been putting "more" of ourselves into our tasks at hand, more muscular tension, more worry, more effort, etc.	Remember, a cold is the body's ingenious way of bringing itself back to balance. Due to busy circumstances in our lives, most of us simply won't allow ourselves proper periods of rest and restoration. Hence, thank your body for showing you what it truly needs to function optimally again. We're only human and the body is only capable of so much. Feldenkrais is great (for prevention) to help the body relearn how to "let go" of excess muscular effort and tension and restore an internal state of calm. Incorporate "slow" practice activities such as reading, meditating, sleeping, reconnecting with old friends, watching feel-good movies, etc. Body/Being Alignment exercise (See the workbook.) Nothing helps a cold better than a good night's sleep!
Colon	Holding on to emotions of the past with a strict internal "rule-book" of how things need to be. Anal-retentive behaviors. "It's got to be this way!"	Most likely the physiology of this person is one that contracts around their buttocks and inner organs. This person may overanalyze things and have a narrow vision of life. Hence, the solution is anything that frees up this pattern in their body and in their mind! Open your perspective and find ok-ness with how things are rather than how they "should" be.

Connective Tissue Disease (See also Autoimmune)	Being eaten alive: "I'm unworthy and in the way. Hence, I need to compensate by doing more and giving more of myself away."	Karmic and familial healing Belief change and inner child healing— Go back in time to when this notion of yourself first originated. Heal that belief. Realize that each time you think such thoughts you are abusing your little one. Hold that little child close to your heart and promise him/ her you'll always be there. Promise him/her you will stop being so cruel.

| Constipation (See Also- "Bloated Belly/Flatulence.") | "I can't let go." Lack of trust in having enough. "I want to push you out of me, but I just can't!" Pent-up anger/irritation and feeling fed up.

Buried shame Beating myself up for all my wrongdoings: "I'm a bad person." "I'm wrong." "I'm not good enough."

Another pattern with people with chronic constipation is they may frequently do things like overeat to then give themselves a good reason to punish themselves later. This way, they'll get their fair dose of the self-flagellating strokes they subconsciously believe they deserve.

"I can allow myself pleasure, yet I'll have to pay the price later. Hence, I may need to sneak it." | Spend time in nature, bringing yourself back to your natural free essence.

Belief change work.

Karmic work: Remember, you are not your past. You are a good person, so stop punishing yourself.

What is it you're holding so tightly on to? What are you hiding?

Ask yourself to your heart: "Why do I feel a need to hide this or keep it secret?" "What would it take for me to let go, to trust more, to allow myself to indulge in the pleasures of life without feeling guilty afterward?"

Affirmation: "It is safe to let go." Or "It's ok to come out." (i.e., with whatever you are hiding).

You have a LOT of light to share with the world. Stop blocking it!

See "Bloated Belly/Flatulence," above. |
|---|---|---|

Covid-19 – 1st Strain (moderate to severe symptoms) More mild versions meaning may be more similar to a cold. Hence, see -"Cold."	Reflection time to examine aspects of your personal character and/or the limits of your own capabilities. 1. Think of this illness as a humility check. You might have the experience of the universe halting everything else in your life (and potentially pulling you backwards), to allow you time and space to reflect upon an aspect of your character which may be beneficial to alter or shift in some way. What might this aspect be? 2. A sudden realization that you are not the "superwoman" (or man) with unlimited capabilities you thought you were. A temporary feeling of self-doubt or failure. Anxiety, worry, and stress may be experienced as a precursor to the onset of symptoms.	Take advantage of this "downtime" to reflect upon how you've been showing up…for your family...for yourself…and for the people whom you interact with on a daily basis. The universe right now is asking you to surrender, soften, and turn in words. Only you can access the information and healing that is necessary, (which is why this condition is one of isolation). How do you want to show up for others? Might there be certain attitudes or behaviors that may be advantageous to shift? If so, how then might other people and the world around you respond differently if these aspects were altered? What if anything is standing in the way? Love the younger version of yourself who may have believed he/she had to figure everything out and know the answers in order to be good enough and loved. Let the little one know that she/he is "good enough" just the way she is. Absorb this notion into your heart.

COPD	Blockage at the base of the throat area that is preventing the energy of the physical body from conjoining with spirit. This occurs at a time when higher purpose and soul divinity are desired yet feel unobtainable.	Stop smoking if you are.

Clear your environment of all dust, chemicals, and fumes. Replace all toxic products such as soaps, shampoos, cleaning products, deodorants, etc., with natural and organic.

Start a practice of incorporating anything that helps you to feel inner peace and the God of your own heart such as walks to the park, spending time with a grandchild, listening to relaxing melodies, meditation, etc. |
| Cough (See Also "Phlegm.") | Barking at the world

Feeling unheard | |

Cramps (See "Menstrual Cramps" or "Abdominal Pain," as appropriate.)	Stopping the flow or process of something. Contractions can be due to upcoming fears.	"What in my life am I fearing or feeling contraction around and why?" "How may I be contracting, or holding on, that is contributing to a block in the flow of my vital fluids (blood, lymph, cellular nutrient exchange, etc.)?" "How may I be contracting, or holding on, that is contributing to a block in the flow of my life?" "What in my life has just occurred or is in the process of occurring that is causing me to use more force or control to achieve my desired outcome?" (See also "Menstral Cramps" and "Abdominal Pain" solutions.)
Cut (Skin)	"I did something wrong." Prior to the action of cutting yourself, you subconsciously left your body. This could be due to overwhelm, overexcitement, narcissism, etc. And cutting provides you the opportunity to reconnect and come back into your body, to feel again. Skin represents a boundary to life. Self-punishment, denying self-pleasure	

CVA/Stroke	"I've had enough." "I'm tired of this!"	The work here is to find a deeper purpose or reason to "stay" that is unrelated to job or career.
	Tired of myself, tired of being the one who always has the answers and "knows."	An aspect of your childhood has been lost and is looking to be found. • At what age did you lose the part of you that would romp around and play freely like a young child?
	In the past, their deep focus on career or some aspect of life may have caused a disassociation with the physical body and now they need to learn the tools to reconnect with it.	• Complete this sentence, "In order to comply with my family's rules, at this age, I needed to ___. " • What did this little ___ -year old want or need? • If there were one thing you could do right now to play more freely like your ___ -year-old child have wanted to, what might that be?
	A desire to leave the body. For some, there is deep tranquility and peace in this place of disassociation and disconnection. A place where you are bathed in white light. .	Spend some time with this little one and see if you can begin to play with her and meet her needs (at least in your imagination). If frustration, irritation, or boredom sets in, remember to be gentler and kinder to yourself. Feldenkrais is great for you, especially as it integrates both hemispheres of your brain and brings you back into your physical body. Body/being connection (See the workbook.) Integration work (See the workbook.) Grounding (See page 179.)

Cyst	Picture-a growth of that which is covering up your light. It looks like a circle covering most of the sun. Increased pressure placed upon you from the outside world that has you respond by using more force and pressure, (especially if this is located on a finger or foot).	Strengthen your feelings of self-worth, significance, and power. What you do doesn't depict who you are. Who you are is not defined by what you do! (Especially if the cyst is located on an organ or inside of you). Belief change work, particularly around effort, obligation, and responsibility. Stress management techniques and anything that will help you to break free of the pressure from the external world and using more force. Soften your fingers as you type and do repetitive tasks.
Diabetes	Gaps in the flow of life-force energy. Sorrow and disappointment for depriving the self of life's "sweetness." "You can't have ____ 'it'." "Life's not about you."	Reconnect with your desire and passion for life. Perform belief change work around your ability to "have" and your "deservingness." Create boundaries from those who might be taking your energy (See workbook). Get into a healthy regimen of diet and exercise. Visualize waking up bright-eyed and excited for the day prior to going to sleep. And then each morning, when you wake up, proclaim out loud, "Today is going to be the best day of my life!" Make NOW count!

Digestion, Difficulty Taking in And Assimilating Foods (See Also "Anorexia," As Appropriate.)	Picture-a person all skin and bones, due to starvation, finding a grain of rice and giving it to a bird or insect. Self-deprivation Difficulty receiving nourishment from others, as well as yourself. Difficulty assimilating life. "I can't stomach this." Lack of deservingness: "I don't deserve."	It is crucial that you begin to reconnect with your self-worth and the planet's need for you. You are a vital and necessary component of existence and humanity waits for you to step forth. Reexamine your coping mechanisms and the unmet needs that lie beneath them. Behaviors such as control, hoarding, and deprivation are all behaviors designed to meet your unmet needs. What are other ways to meet your needs, specifically your emotional needs? Ideally, we want to be in symbiotic flow with the universe around us, giving freely and allowing ourselves to become "filled up." To do this, we must work through any limiting beliefs around being unworthy or not deserving. Perform any activity that reconnects you with love and your innate self-worth.
Disabilities	Deep love and loyalty toward family, taking on their unfortunate fate in order to help them to evolve or grow	

Dupuytren's Contracture	"I need to hold on."	Reflect upon what you are holding tightly onto, literally and metaphorically. What would it take for you to "let go" and trust just a little bit more?
Dyslexia	Picture-walking through a labyrinth or maze as opposed to taking the straight path. "I'm confused." "I'm lost." "I don't know which way to go." Feelings of helplessness Inability to move forward.	Belief change work in regard to feeling powerful, confident, and self-sufficient. Self-acceptance Walking Your Path exercise (See the workbook.) Anything that will help you to take that next step forward and feel safe and enabled is the way to go. Goal setting can help, as can cleanliness and organization. Ask your higher self: "What might you be getting out of this state of being lost and confused?

Edema	Incapable: "I can't." Self-imposed limitations. Bottled-up fears. Feeling trapped or numb. Blocking the flow of life.	Massage your body parts with a technique called "retrograde massage." To do this: 1. Apply a thick massage cream to the body part. 2. Place your fingertips on the opposite arm at the most distal (away from your heart) part. 3. Provide gentle inward pressure with your fingertips as you slide your fingers in the direction toward your heart (distally to proximally). 4. Allow the massage cream to move your fingers, as opposed to you moving it. Soften your fingers (so they're not straight or overworking). Go so slow that an observer could hardly notice any movement. 5. As you do this, think to yourself the following affirmation: "I allow myself to re-assimilate the fluids of life." Belief change work or anything that will help you to move through the limitations, as described.
Elbow, Left (For a Left-Handed Individual, This Info. Can Be Switched with The Right.)	Minding your own business Self-protection	(See "Elbow-Medial Epicondylitis.")

Elbow, Right (For a Right-Handed Individual, This Info. Can Be Switched with The Left.)	Pushing things away unconsciously while feeling the need to "do."	Journal about what it is that you most want yet maybe somehow unconsciously pushing away. Practice the art of "being," rather than "doing." Take more frequent pause breaks.

Elbow-Lateral Epicondylitis (Or Tennis Elbow)	Picture-your arm held out in front of you in the "stop" position in an attempt to keep an aspect of the world out. "Stand back!" "Get away!" (Please note this pattern is extremely subtle, as people with this syndrome are far from dramatic.) Often people with a more frequent occurrence of this syndrome have a longer humorous (upper arm bone). For this reason, an ergonomic consultation can be beneficial to ensure that your workstation is a good fit for you.	Meditate on what possibly you may be wanting to push away and why. This might even be happening subconsciously. Is there anyone or anything you had this pattern with during your earlier years of life? With the notion that "what you resist persists," is there anything you can do to release such resistance? Apply a tennis elbow band or strap (which you can pick up at any drug-store or grocery store) and secure it two finger-widths below your elbow. Two minutes three times a day of circular ice massage on this region of your elbow with an ice cup (water frozen into a Dixie cup). Due to your anthropometric measurements and habits, your shoulder-blade region and back may be less engaged with the movements of your arm, resulting in overuse of the muscles of your distal arm. (If this is so, perform the Foam Roller exercises from my book, *A Quick Guide to Easing Pain/* also in my *Comfort for Life* DVD.) Feldenkrais lessons that focus on the integration of the arm with the rest of the shoulder girdle and back can also be beneficial.
Elbow Medial Epicondylitis (Cubital Tunnel Region)	What is it you are holding onto the tightest right now in your life? What would it take to release this hold just a little bit more?	When you sleep, put your hand inside a pillowcase to prevent yourself from flexing your arm into a fetal or flexed position.

Elbow Tingling And/or Numbness (Also See "Edema" or Paresthesia," if Appropriate)	Picture-a surfer-looking dude with shoulder-length dirty-blond hair, forearms resting on the table, slouching, in a sitting position, uninspired with the work he is doing (representing a distant archetype in you that is peaking through). Numbing yourself and checking out on the world. "It doesn't matter."	Meditate upon when, hypothetically, as a little girl or boy the specific behaviors and actions you took to receive love and attention from your parents felt unsuccessful. • Did you eventually give up trying and rather take on the perspective of "It just doesn't matter"? • What is at the root of this emotional void for this little one? • What was he/she lacking? • Ask the little one, what might he/she need to fill it? • How might this pertain to your present-time life? • What in your current life might give you more of a reason to be alive and present?
Endometriosis	Loneliness, void, disappointment, loss. I'm here but nobody gets me, I can easily blend into the background. Unhealed emotions from the inner child.	Belief Change and Inner Child Healing. (See the workbook)
Eye Issues (See "Vision," Below.)	Difficulty or fear of seeing the future (a feeling of impending doom). Or Resistance to being "in the body" and seeing your own reality.	

Fibroids	Picture-a circle representing you with a bunch of other circles eagerly toppling one another to get closer to you to leech or feed off your energy and nutrients. "I need to sacrifice myself for the good of others." Sacrificing your own needs. Isolation, being overwhelmed, exhaustion, responsibility, overexertion, putting the needs of others ahead of your own.	Belief Change/Inner Child healing, Boundaries and Cutting Cords exercises (See workbook). Free yourself from the excessive feeling of responsibility and obligation. See my YouTube video, *How to Expand Time*. Affirmation: "I have time and space for me."

Fibromyalgia	Energies, voices, people from the past, all competing to take refuge in your body. Irritation, body discomfort, and hyper-sensitivity, especially with fluctuations in noise, temperature, and certain tactile sensations. This person will have difficulty differentiating other voices from that of their own and hence will be in a constant tug-of-war until their own voice becomes senior. "Get away from me." "The world's responsibility is weighing on me." "I'll handle it." "I'll suffer, so you don't have to." A need to isolate, to move away from it all.	The goal for this person is to take ownership and authority over your entire space and quiet all those competing voices inside of you so there is one, and only one, that presides, that of your own, and to release the responsibility and suffering of others (which you have subconsciously been carrying). Imagine entering a conference room. Ask all the competing voices inside you (spirit, mother, husband, etc.) to stand over at one side of the room. Let them know you will call upon them, one by one, as needed, yet for right now, it's you, and only you, leading the classroom. (See Prayer Before Bed page 178.) Create healthy boundaries with people in your life so you no longer feel the need to push anyone or anything away. Instead, replace this with an energy that feels good inside (See Boundaries exercise in the workbook). Feldenkrais to let go of the excess muscle tension and effort you might be using for everyday tasks such as getting out of bed and cooking. Update the contract with Spirit to no longer take on the suffering of others (See the Calling back your Energy exercise in Workbook). Ancestral and karmic healing.
Fingers, Joints/Nodes /Swelling, etc.	Blocks on the path, particularly as it pertains to creativity and doing your craft out in the world.	

Fingers, Stabbing Sensations	Picture-your hand taking a knife out of your back and sticking it into someone else. "I'll stab you, so I don't have to keep stabbing myself." Blaming others, difficulty regulating the energy in your life, overtaxing oneself.	

Finger Tingling (In A Localized Region, One Finger) (See "Pinky," If Applicable. If Ringling in Numerous Areas, See "Paresthesia.")	Control, fear of losing control "It's got to be this way." Excess pressure on self around expectations, deadlines, etc.	The most prominent factors are typing, writing, etc., while habitually (and unconsciously) hyper-extending the fingers. It can also be in conjunction with the forceful use of your fingers such as pounding keys while typing or performing heavy construction work. It is recommended to keep a slight bend in each of the three joints of the fingers and soften the use of each one. Avoid a tight grip, especially with vibratory tools. What in your life might you be exerting excessive control around, and/or what might you be putting excessive pressure on yourself around?
Foot, Internal Rotation (For Instance., Toes Pointed Inward)	"I'm turning in on me."	Anything that can help you to open up more to the world with your love and light.

Foot, External Rotation (For Instance, Toes Pointed Outward)	A drive to put more of self forward to be available for love and attention: "Love me, see me."	
Left Foot	Picture-your left foot getting stuck, so you are unable to move forward like the rest: Settling (for less) "Everyone else is moving on without me." "Stay away." Staying stuck in the past.	
Foot Fracture	Self-flagellating thoughts/anger that is causing a lack of stability, support, and grounding.	
Foot, Sole of Foot (For Instance, Plantar Fasciitis)	Picture-stomping your foot down. "I'm one step removed." Lacking connection with the earth and those closest to you.	This is your opportunity to connect deeper with those around you. Make eye contact and ask them questions that help them to share more about themselves, for instance, "What was your favorite part of ____?" "What are the biggest challenges you are facing in your life right now?" Grounding (page 179).
Foot/Ankle Sprain/Twisting	Cross motives, for instance, saying one thing, but thinking and feeling another	

Foot Fungus	Feeling unsupported by the weight of the earth.

Difficulty trusting the steps you take and walking your path.

Picture-turning your back or running from beliefs of the past until you can no longer run anymore. They'll creep up and get ya.

Stagnating beliefs from the past. | Affirmation: "I am moving forward in life."

Remember to take all of yourself forward, even the parts you want to reject and leave behind. (See Parts Integration in the workbook.)

See Grounding suggestions (page 179). |
| Gums | Picture-the earth eroding beneath your feet.

Gums represent your foundation of safety and security. | Encourage anything that helps you to reclaim a sense of security and safety.

See Grounding suggestions (page 179). |
| Hair Loss
(See "Balding or alopecia.") | | |

Hand (Palm Area) Hand pad, (Thumb and pinky eminences)	Blocks on your creative output (creating things with your hands), most likely due to unexpressed emotions held in your chest such as irritation, frustration, and angst. Feeling stuck or confused. vigilance, self-protection, fear	Anything it will take for you to move through such stuck emotions like journaling, talking to a health professional, sharing your feelings with a friend, driving fast down a highway and screaming out the window, etc. Emotional Body exercises (See workbook). Soften your fingers as you write, paint, and perform all fine motor activities. Imagine gold light energy flowing from your chest down your arms and out through your fingertips, down your legs and into the earth. This is your vital energy. Meditate on this continuous flow of light throughout your body. -- Anything to release this fear and trauma response in your body. Having the strength to say STOP!
Hand, Web Space	"Stop." Feeling stuck in a web "I can't get out."	

Headache-(General) (See Also "Vertigo" When Dizziness Is Involved.)	• Picture # 1: A disarray of lines forming a helical mesh around your frontal cortex, like vines strangulating the brain. • Picture #2: A young child or infant trying to solve the issues of Mom and Dad and make sense of the world around them. "The pressures never stop." "I need to figure this one out." Trying to make sense of it all. "I'm lost." "I need to find my way out of here." "This is a lot to handle." "This is too much." "I'm overwhelmed." A headache could also occur as a result of referred pain when the original source of it stems from a block in your throat chakra/self-expression. Anger/frustration	Do anything you can do to stop the monkey mind of thought and relax your eyes, such as taking a nap, lying down, being kind and loving to yourself. Take the pressure off, release control, and quiet your "analyzer," the part of you that needs to figure it all out. Do know that taking these mini breaks will help you to be more efficient and productive in the long run. Relaxing herbal essences such as lavender, chamomile, kava kava, holy basil, and vanilla White willow bark Any processing or inner child/belief change work needs to occur at a time when symptoms are alleviated. Visualize that to the degree you are holding the world, the world is also holding you back. Affirmation: "The world is holding me. It is safe to let go."

Headaches, Cluster or High-Intensity	The picture is the same as Picture #1, above, yet I see even more globs or clusters of these mesh bundles. The analytical processes of the mind are constantly firing, even at rest. For these individuals, being in their body is generally uncomfortable, and hence, they'll choose to busy themselves with work, responsibilities, or pain symptoms.
Headache (Constant)	Same as above "If I just keep myself in a constant state of figuring things out, we will then be safe and protected."
Heart Attack	Denial or squeezing out love and joy often in exchange for money or stature.
Heart Surgery (Open)	"Stay away." "Stay back." Powerlessness, vulnerability, protecting self.

Herpes (Genital)	Picture-hopping with bare feet across hot rocks (representing all the areas of shame), too hot to be touched. Second picture-standing on a small piece of ice floating on a lake, fearing getting off your "small island." Self-blame, shame, sexual guilt, and the need for punishment, self-deprivation and isolation. Emotions are stifled and held inwards. Wanting to Push other people's energy away. Feeling misunderstood and hurt by others. "I don't deserve."	Belief Change/Inner Child Healing (See workbook). Anything to heal your wounds around your shame, sexuality, and guilt. Heal whatever is causing your subconsciou urge to push away others energy as well as the compressive layer of pain that surrounds you. Widen your aura around you, imagine it to be more spacious like a cloud. Cutting Cords (See workbook). Self-acceptance & self-love Affirmation: "I matter."

Hip Pain	Left side: Fear of moving forward, nothing to move forward toward. Right side: Pushing forward	Belief change work Feldenkrais Walking Path exercise (See the workbook.) Left side: What right now is blocking your path forward? What do you fear? What can be done to help you move forward? Right side: Where in your life might you be "pushing" or exerting too much effort? How might you metaphorically walk this path with more ease?
HIV	Picture-a snake/serpent traveling up the middle and right side of the individual's spine and his/her bloodstream filling it with a smoky black color. The head of the serpent circled around his/her neck, pulling his/her back, preventing him/her from moving forward out of the darkness and into the light. Unworthiness, shame: "Every time I shine my light, it's just going to be dimmed down anyway."	Duplication technique: 1. Imagine a snake on one side of yourself (if you identify with this imagery, if not, use an image you identify with). 2. Put a grounding cord on it so it won't get away from you. 3. In your imagination duplicate the snake. Make an exact replica. 4. Smack the two together and have them explode into a million pieces. 5. Release all the pieces and any residual energy away and out of your space. 6. Repeat this three times to help them to disappear completely. 7. Lastly, there should be an empty space on the side of you where the snake energy once was. Fill this space with your high gold. Belief change work Reclaim your personal power and seniority.

Hypersensitivity to Electromagnetic Fields (EMFs) And Environmental Pollutants.	Hypersensitive emotions as a child, hence, you learned to build up an energetic wall of protection around yourself "They're coming in to get me." "It wasn't me." Feeling victimized. "People don't get it." Feeling misunderstood.	Work through trust issues. Grow your confidence and seniority, as the master of your space, allowing only the energy and beings that have your highest good in mind to enter and command all the others to leave (See Prayer Before Bed page 178). Healing around familial beliefs that were passed on to you around fears, worries, and the ways things "need" to be. Who or what is it you are truly protecting yourself from? Who or what might be coming in to get you (literally or metaphorically)? Journal about this. Boundary work (See workbook). Affirmations: "It is safe to be here (in your body)," "The world around me is safe." "I can open my heart to love."
Infections	Picture-a gopher wanting to go down into the gopher hole and get away from_____. "You're irritating me." "I'm going to go back into this hole where it's safe and hide." Denying your own needs Powerlessness and annoyance.	

Itchy Skin (Chronic)	Discomfort from the inside, going against the grain. irritation from others. "Get it out." "I want it to get away."	Cutting cord exercise (See the workbook). Withhold exercise (See the workbook.) Take a bath with calming oils, oatmeal or colloidal oatmeal, or baking soda, etc.
Joints	Lack of flexibility (particularly around the changing tides of life).	Flexibility and surrender are your two key ingredients!
Kidney	Grieving the past: "I don't want to let go." "I need to keep holding on." "Fearing the future."	Grief support and healing. Feldenkrais or any somatic practices that bring you into your body. Grounding practices (See page 179). Body/Being and Emotional Release exercises in the Workbook. Affirmations: "I have everything I need within." "I am going to be ok." "It is safe to let go."

| Knee | Instability and difficulty feeling supported. | Inner-child and belief change work to heal the root of the issues.

Anything that has you feeling more grounded and connected to the earth and more stable within yourself, regardless of circumstances.

See walking your path exercise in the workbook.

Stand about hips-width apart, either barefoot or wearing socks only. Check-in if your energy is leaning back or forward. Is your weight more in your toes or more in your heels? Without bending your knees, slowly lean forward to rock all of your weight into your toes. Then lean back so all of your weight shifts to your heels. Go back and forth slowly shifting your weight and your awareness between your heels and your toes. Then stop and find your weight balanced between the two extremes. This is the place where you want to meet the world, from your power center.

Feldenkrais focused on the back, foot, and legs.

Affirmations: "The earth beneath my feet supports me. I am supported." "I am clear and aligned." |
|---|---|---|

Knee-Rigidity or locking of the knees	**Rigidity or locking** of the knees is associated with a fear of isolation and the need to protect and guard themselves. "I can't move." "I'm stuck." "I can't go forward in life." "I can't do it all alone." "If I don't make it, I'm a failure." Self-doubt	Affirmation: "I walk my path with ease." See "knee" above.
Knee Ligament	At a crossroads, indecision, confusion, self-doubt	Affirmation: "I move as one." (See also "Ligament" suggestions, below.) See "knee" above.
Knee Meniscus	Wanting to leap full throttle forward, yet the universe pulls you back.	Affirmation: "Right here is where I need to be." See "knee" above.
Learning Disorder	Doubting your own capabilities, and hence, unconsciously putting constructs in the way.	Find a practitioner who will continue to praise you for your capabilities and wins, someone who doesn't buy the story of "I can't do it." Spend time with people who are able to deeply see you and believe in you. Focus on what you are good at and fill more of your life up with that. Anything that builds confidence, grounding, seniority, and belief in yourself.

Leg	Right leg: Stiffness, hesitation to walk forward in life, stagnation or overexertion/forcefulness to move forward. Left leg: Blocks on taking your creative and emotional side forward with you.	(See "Sciatic Pain.")
Ligament (See "Knee Ligament" if Appropriate)	Rejecting a certain part of yourself: "Get away." Self-doubt: The ligament is the bridge that connects you to an aspect of yourself that you want to push away or move forward from. The laxity of the ligaments represents stretching that part away from you.	What aspect of yourself might you want to push or move away from? What can you do to be more loving and accepting of this part? Parts Integration (See the exercise in the workbook.) See "Knee Ligament."
Liver	Internalized anger and resentment. "Now look what you left me with." "Now look what you've done."	Transmute these feelings, over time, to understanding, compassion, and when you're ready, forgiveness. Allow yourself to move through the anger through numerous techniques and modalities, for instance, emotional release exercises, journaling, and the other anger management suggestions from this book or elsewhere.

| Lungs | Picture-a house in the middle of the Dust Bowl spinning around and around. Over time, as the dust begins to settle, despair or sadness may set in.

The lungs appear with a dark gray/off-black-colored smoke screen in and around the lungs.

Ungrounded and unsettledness, regret, a feeling of claustrophobia, suffocation, or constriction.
"I am suffocating emotionally."
"I have no space to breathe."
An inability to breathe in life.
Self-doubt.
"If I don't make it, I'm a failure." | Commit to having more loving and intimate relationships in your life.

Anything to bring in more joy, peacefulness, and a feeling of spaciousness into your life.

Breathing exercises can help to create a feeling of spaciousness inside of you.

Massage between each rib gently while relaxing on your back (with your arm supported for comfort). Start toward your sternum, and with two fingers, softly and slowly massage in a circular motion like tracing a dime, out toward your armpit region. Pause to feel the expansion and openness.

Consider a diffuser or vaporizer with grounding essential oils.

Practice being in the now and enjoying the gift of the moment.

Emotional Body exercises in the workbook. |

Lyme Disease	Picture-a desert scene. You are unable to see the dark energy (ticks/Lyme) creeping up behind you, ready to leech out onto you out of your desperation for companionship. Feelings of isolation, aloneness: "Help me, I can't find my way." Feeling incapable: "I'm not capable of doing anything." "I can't do it." "I'm not enough." This is what invites in this leech-like entity, which then leads to "Get off of me" and "Get away from me." Hence, the dichotomy exists: "I can't do it alone and no one can help me." Codependency, where it's too difficult to ask for your needs to be met, hence, you subconsciously, through the "back door," get people to meet them, rather than finding a way to meet them yourself.	Cording exercise: Who specifically do you experience boundary-pushing with to the point that you want them off and out of your space? (See the workbook.) Boundary work (See workbook). Heal the beliefs of being incapable and alone (See workbook). Reclaim your sovereignty.

Melanoma	Scratch that ounce of imperfection away.	"I am enough, just the way I am."
Menstrual Cramps (See Also "PMS," "Cramps," and "Abdominal Pain.")	(Just prior to the cramps setting in), picture a bombardment of electrical activity in the air, causing particles to be in entropy and disarray and a roar of the waves of the ocean (the size of the waves depends on the intensity of the cramps). The electrical activity came as a result of stress, constantly being on the go, as well as pressure on yourself. "I'm ready for battle." Once cramps begin, sadness and shutting, or slowing down.	Go gentle on yourself. We all need to take a day of rest, and because so many of us don't allow our bodies to do so, the Almighty has brought this day upon us. You are granted one day of rest, like a monthly Sabbath. If your schedule allows, perform any "slow practice" activities today such as reading a book, appreciating a work of art, writing, inner reflection, doing crafts, and meditating. "Today is the day I get to return to the place of self-love." Meditation: Imagine a bright golden sun shining above you. Imagine it smoothing out the waves of the ocean, as you would spread frosting on a cake. Continue to smooth it out until the waves have become relaxed and calm.
Menstruation, Heavy, "Menorrhagia"	Releasing of that storm (mentioned above), a cleansing and clearing process that restores homeostatic balance. The body's call for more attention. Rejection of the feminine.	

Mold Toxicity	Picture-walls caving in around you. Tightness around lower-throat/upper-chest region. "Why even start if you're never going to make it anyway?" "Good things happen, yet they will soon be taken away". "Getting closer, yet then something sets me back." Lack of deserving "I can't do this anymore." "I'm over it!" Self-protection/guarding With a cough and cold symptoms, you are expelling the toxic belief systems you inherited as a child.	Belief change/inner-child work to cultivate the belief that you do deserve, for instance, a good job, loving relationships, family. You do deserve pleasure, happiness, laughter, and joy! Boundary work (See Workbook). Eventually, you want to get to a place where you don't feel so burdened or overwhelmed by other people and the world around you, where you feel free of the desire to push others away. Meditate and imagine a beautiful spacious house. Paint the inside a beautiful rose color, gold, or milky-white, or whatever color most resonates with you. Fill your home with this color vibration and warmth. Imagine fresh air and oxygen circulating through the house. Get a vaporizer, diffuser, or anything that will help you to fill your lungs with fresh air. Allow yourself to fully exhale. Affirmations: "There is a perfect place for me." "The world is safe." "I deserve it." Grounding exercises (See page 179).
Mucus (See "Phlegm.")		

Muscular Dystrophy (Limb Girdle)	"I can't get ahead." Hence the mind overthinks ways in which it can. A disconnection from the lower body. Rejection of the physical body.	Belief change/inner child healing See Body/Being exercise in the workbook.
Neck Knot	Overusing the mental/logical mind in combination with "overdoing" and rigid thinking.	Pelvic Tilt/Neck Release exercise: 1. Lie on your back on a fairly firm surface with your knees bent. 2. Wad up a washcloth and place it under the area where the knot is. You may need to roll your body slightly to the side if the knot is on the side of your neck. 3. Position yourself so your nose is in line with your chin and belly button and you're laying directly on the area where the knot is located. 4. Gently push through both feet just enough to roll your tailbone up (and your low back will flatten), as you perform small, gentle, pelvic tilts. Continue the tilts in a slow rhythmic manner. Close your eyes, relax your muscles. As you roll up, you should feel gentle pressure where the knot touches the towel. 5. Incorporate the wine bottle cork in your mouth technique if you find your mouth/jaw region tensing. 6. After doing about 7-15 pelvic tilts, remove the washcloth, lie on your back, and feel the increased ease and range of motion on that side. (See my YouTube video, *Easing Neck Pain*. This exercise is also in my book, *A Quick Guide to Easing Pain*.) See suggestions for "Neck Stiffness," below.

Neck/Head Protruding Forward of Body.	Picture-a mother walking by her little boy with little or slight acknowledgment of him. The little boy wants more love and affection from the mother, and she gives him just enough to keep him wanting more. Wanting, eagerness: "Love me." Looking forward/needing to "do" more, driving faster or harder	Your life-long mission will be to receive more love and affirmation. However, you'll likely be facing the "hungry ghost syndrome." Even when it is given to you, your beliefs that you're not worthy of receiving it may block the actual experience of it, and hence leave you hungry for more. Hence, this is what you need to focus on for the belief change exercises. Start to believe that you are worthy and capable of receiving all the love in the world and getting filled up and nourished. (See the belief change exercises in the workbook and on my YouTube channel.) The true healing will come when you fill yourself up with so much self-love that you will no longer need to receive it from the outside. Neck Feldenkrais exercises (See my YouTube video, *Easing Neck Pain*. also, my book, *A Quick Guide to Easing Pain*.)
Neck Rounded Forward and/or Down with a Protruding T1 Region	Shame, feelings of inadequacy: "Something is wrong with me." It's common for this person to hide from these emotions in activities such as work.	What is it you are hiding from, feeling shame around, feeling unworthy about? Where did these emotions and feelings initially come from? This is where to begin the healing. Learn to love that wounded yet perfectly innocent inner child. Neck Feldenkrais exercises, (See my YouTube video, *Easing Neck Pain*. Also see my book, *A Quick Guide to Easing Pain*.) *or* See Pelvic Tilt/Neck Release exercise under "Neck Knot" above.

Neck (Posterior)- Straight Cervical Spine (See Also "Neck Stiffness.")	Skepticism, hyper-vigilance Fearing what's out there and what the world is going to throw at you next. Picture #1: All fingers pointing at you. Picture #2: A young child hiding in the corner watching a parent in distress and embracing/fearing for their safety, wondering what he should do. Dodging the bullet: "It wasn't me." Guilt, responsibility. a need to be on alert! These people will also have neck stiffness as well.	Travel back to your earliest memories of when you might have experienced such emotions. Perform inner-child healing. Ask yourself the following questions: • What were my primary concerns and fears at that time? • What was the mechanism I embraced to find safety and security during these times when I experienced the world as unsafe? • How does it present in my physical body? • How might this coping mechanism have served me at that time? • How might it still be serving me now? • What might be going on in my world right now that correlates to my first answer? • What are some things I can do to change the way it presents at a physical level in my body today? • What are some things I can do today to change my emotional response to such events? • How does my little inner child want to be loved? Practice softening your eyes as you go throughout your day. Roll up a washcloth or hand towel and place it under your first two cervical vertebra and perform the pelvic tilt exercise as explained under "Neck Knot" above. Or see instructions in my Neck YouTube videos or *A Quick Guide to Easing Pain* book.

Neck Stiffness/ tightness on the side of neck, (See also "Neck/Shoulder Stiffness.")	Picture-a man steering a ship, thinking there's only one way to go, only seeing straight ahead on the course of travel, not seeing the ocean that resides all around. Left side: A resistance or fear of looking at the past: "I can't look back." Right side: Lack of flexibility, not open to seeing all the options: "This is the way to do it."	Left side – Heal wounds and sorrows of the past so there is more ease in looking back. Right side - Expand your flexibility of thought and perspective. Expanding your peripheral vision will help to increase your neck comfort and range of motion. (For techniques, see my book, *A Quick Guide to Easing Pain.*) Feldenkrais towel roll under neck exercise series: • Lie on your back with your knees bent on a fairly firm surface. • Very gently roll your head to the right, then to the left, just so you can distinguish the amount of easy range of motion to both sides. • Roll onto your right side. Roll up a hand towel and place it under your first two cervical vertebras (upper neck). • Bend your left knee and stand that foot a comfortable distance from your pelvis. • Push through the left foot just enough to perform small gentle rhythmic pelvic tilts. Make note if you're tensing and contracting anywhere you don't need to, for instance, your jaw. If so, soften and release these areas. • Perform about 10 one-legged pelvic tilts, then move the towel roll down one vertebra and perform 10 more pelvic tilts. Go lighter, easier, softer. • Roll onto your back, relax, and compare the differences. (See the lesson on my YouTube video, *Easing Neck Pain.* also, my book, *A Quick Guide to Easing Pain.*)

Neck/Shoulder (Upper Trapezium) Stiffness (With Shoulder Raised Up Toward Ear) (It Can Be with Radiating Pain.)	Pressure to be a certain way and achieve a particular outcome. "This is the way it needs to be." (For some people) - the need to "put a foot in your mouth." Hence, it may be better not to say anything at all. Protection of thyself.	Quiet your fast and determined mind, widen your peripheral vision, and open your heart to other people's perspectives. More ease and flexibility in your body & in your mind (less effort). Soften your jaw, allow a slight parting of your teeth, for instance, when at the computer. (Placing a wine cork between your lips for five minutes is a great way to ease this tension.) See "Neck Stiffness," above.
Nerves (See "Paresthesia.")	Picture-energy congested in the torso and not traveling through the arms (or all four extremities). Locked-down frustration and unexpressed emotions that want to seep out. Depletion of nutrients. The vending machine is now empty and needs to be restocked. "I need to be replenished." "I need to be refilled." Depletion caused by fear, overwhelm, confusion, and over contracting your muscles to "hold on." Perfectionism. Pressure to do better. Deprivation.	

Obesity and Overeating	Picture-molecules of sensation bombarding under the confines of the skin representing stuck creative potential. "I'm too much." "I'm invisible." "I'm not enough." "No man can truly handle me." Issues of control, self-deprivation, locked-up anger, and resentment Craving love and closeness yet convinced that you won't get it. Hence, using fat around your body to simulate such feelings, providing a false layer of comfort and security, and using food as a substitute for a feeling of affection. The result of feeling unseen or invisible as a child resulted in their need to grow themselves bigger as then, maybe, just maybe, "then I will be seen." Holding in other people's emotions and taking too much responsibility for others.	It is essential to excavate and reconnect with these locked-up emotions and feelings. • What is the need or nutrient that is not being met? • Express your feelings in writing specifically around loneliness and feeling unloved or speak it out loud to either a friend, a trained professional, or someone who can provide a supportive ear. Withhold exercise, inner-child and belief change work, and cutting cords (See these exercises in the workbook.) Release the burdens of responsibility and guilt you have been holding on to for way too long. Choose exercises and activities you enjoy doing. Find a walking or exercise buddy to help keep you motivated and accountable. A pre-planned three-meal/day healthy diet is ideal to help regulate your metabolism and hypothalamus (hunger and satiation center) and decrease emotional eating. Stock your refrigerator and cabinets with healthy snack options such as celery and carrot sticks, apples with tahini or almond butter, etc. Get rid of the sweet temptations. One reward food per day is fine, yet if you're someone who is unable to stop at just one, eliminate them from your household completely.

OCD (Obsessive Compulsive Disorder)	Picture #1: Walking into a completely dark cave in the ground and trying to find your way around. Picture #2: Mother (or the one who's love as an infant you most wanted) turned her back to you. Hence, as an infant, you had to find "find your own way." "I'm lost. I can't find my way." The compulsion to constantly move in order to avoid feeling the emotional void of being unloved and unwanted. "It needs to be perfect; then she'll see me and love me."	
Ovarian Cancer (See "Cancer.")		
Parasites	Allowing your energy to be parasited on. Giving your energy to others. Powerlessness, hopelessness, helplessness, anxiety, worry.	Cording exercise (See workbook). Anything that helps you to claim your power, confidence, and seniority. Reconnect with that which inspires and excites you.

Paresthesia/Tingling, Burning, Numbness in Fingers and Spotty Regions of Your Arms and Hands (For Pinky Side Hand Only, See "Pinky," below.)	(See "Nerve," above.) Deprivation, abandonment, self-flagellating thoughts, control	When symptoms are bilateral (in both arms), and don't follow a direct nerve pathway, they are almost always of cervical origin. Only a few diseases may be exceptions to this rule. (Hence, see also "Neck" suggestions.) Feldenkrais lessons. However, keep in mind that your tolerance and patience for each lesson may be decreased. So, don't overdo it; listen to what your body is asking for at every step. When performing such lessons, if you experience a temporary increase in paresthesia symptoms, most likely this simply means your nervous system is resisting the surrender and letting-go process. This holding-on and controlled state that I speak of is familiar and your body is tricking you into believing that this state is better. It's important to reprogram such beliefs and physiological patterns. The Feldenkrais method can help with this. Belief change work (See Workbook or YouTube). Medical interventions such as nerve blocks, medications, etc., can be effective at providing symptom relief and healing. Yet, at the same time, they will prevent you from really feeling your emotional body and the wounds that lie beneath. Healing will be most effective when therapeutic modalities are used in conjunction with interpersonal work, perhaps with a professional who can help you to fill the void between what your physical body knows so well, control, fear, and holding on, versus safety, trust, and surrender, and forming a new relationship with the pain/pleasure conundrum and perfectionist ideals.

Parkinson's	Picture-*clang, clang, clang,* pots banging at one's head. "The noise and stimulation from outside are so loud and disturbing that I need to come inside where it's safe and warm." Vision and gait only as wide as the narrow doorway from where he resides. "The world outside is unsafe." "I need to have full control."	Low stimulation, grounded type of environments, for instance, soft, gentle music. Breathing, meditation Peripheral vision exercise (See my book, *A Quick Guide to Easing Pain,* for more details.) Anything that will help you to surrender control, soften, and release your grip on life. Feldenkrais!
Pelvis (Stiff Or Painful)	Picture-the Tin Man in *The Wizard of Oz.* A need to hold the pelvis stiff in order to keep it all together. Cautious.	

Phlegm/ Mucus	Holding on to old patterns and experiences from the past that want to be upchucked and expelled. Suppressed anger and frustration for not being heard and feeling misunderstood. "I don't care" (surrendering to the fight). The throat being the bardo between the physical and spiritual plane, the old, and the new.	During illnesses such as the flu, colds, and pneumonia, phlegm becomes more excessive in an attempt to get rid of the bacteria or viral particles within the body. Hence, see treatment suggestions (viruses or colds if appropriate). Release that which isn't serving you at this present time, be it in the emotional or physical realm. See the workbook for the Cutting Cords, Withholds, and Emotional Body Exercises.

Pinky- or Ulnar-Sided Hand and Finger Pain	Picture-a woman shaking her pinky at someone as if to say, "No no, I didn't say you could do that." Moral compass of right versus wrong. Fear of losing control and feeling powerless. Dismissing the feminine (with the perspective that bending at each joint of the hand represents weakness, surrender, the feminine). Over-dominance of the masculine (in a female body).	Notice if your tendency is to have your wrist deviating toward the pinky side and your pinky hyper-extended (straight) during tasks such as computer use. Keep your wrist and pinky in neutral, which means your third finger is in line with the middle of your wrist, and your fingers in a relaxed "C" shape, with a slight bend in each finger joint. This is especially important during activities such as typing on the computer (See my book, *A Quick Guide to Easing Pain,* for more details.) Write the word *masculine* on a piece of paper. Then, as a stream-of-consciousness exercise, write down all the words that instantly come to mind when you think this word. Next, do the same for the word *feminine*. Notice any judgments that came up for you around the word *feminine*. Do the same for the word *woman*, and then *man*. Notice what in your life you are gripping on to, and ask yourself if it's possible to let go just a little bit more Soften and reconnect with your feminine essence. The receptive, the creative, the nurturer. Smell a flower and appreciate the fragrance, speak your feelings from your heart, perform all of your movements with softness and grace.
Poison Oak or Ivy	Scratching away someone or something's energy that is in your space "I want my space." Scratching their energy away.	

Prostate Cancer	Loss of power and energy flow (such as what a man may initially experience after he retires).	Ask yourself: "What personal need in my life is missing (for instance, feeling of importance and being needed)?" Make a list of opportunities and possibilities for how you could go about filling such needs. Expand your mind to new possibilities for how you can achieve a feeling of success and accomplishment. Perhaps it's even from spending time with a grandchild.
PMS (Premenstrual Syndrome) (See Also "Menstrual Cramps" And "Menstruation.").	Picture-water molecules heating up and flying around, bombarding against one another. It could be the start of an electrical storm. (Yet one may confuse this inner discomfort for outer discomfort.) Irritation, annoyance, confusion (See "Mental Cramps.")	Release other people's energy the best you can and avoid taking anything too personally. Cutting cords exercise (See my YouTube channel or the exercise in the workbook.) This too shall pass! See "Menstrual Cramps."

Psoriasis (See Also "Itchy Skin")	The picture is one of dark energy around your upper body representing other people and entities on and around you, suffocating you. "You're taking my identity away." Irritation toward another (likely either your mother or a lover). "Get it away!" Responsibilities: "It's too much." "I can't deal." Scratching it all away.
Raynaud's Phenomenon	Lack of vitality Nervous system stuck in a freeze response, pulling in toward your core. "It's safer in here." (Energy is locked up in the chest/torso area and is unable to flow past your shoulders and pelvic region.)

| Reflux (See Also "Throat Congestion") | Controlling the direction of life's flow: "I need to hold it all in." Pressure on self: "This is how it's going to be." Picture #1: Two large blocks or stones are placed on the road on either side of your car, preventing it from turning or passing through. The easy way through would be to turn your car just before the second block, yet being the high achiever that you are, moving so fast, you miss that turn. Picture #2: Beaver dam, each stick put there, one at a time, yet when they accumulate, it creates a dam blocking the flow of water from flowing through. Picture #3: Sands of an hourglass—the middle of the hourglass represents your throat and the pressure that surrounds it preventing the sand from easily flowing through. Each of these pictures represents a block of the flow of energy right in the center of the throat. The flow is blocked going downward and the energy from below accumulates to the point where it has no choice but to reflexively (like a geyser) jut upward. (See "Throat Congestion"). | Anything that will help you to take life's pressures away and help you to surrender to life's flow. Let go of idealization about how things "should" be. Cutting cords (See my YouTube channel or the exercise in the workbook.) (See suggestions for "Digestion" and "Constipation," as appropriate.) |

Repetitive Stress of the Entire Arm/Hand/Wrist (See also "Paresthesias")	Picture-fingers/arms exerting, working hard over the computer screen. Energy is all up in the head and ignoring the body. Insignificance and unworthiness: Self-worth is tied to what you do as opposed to who you are. Strong moral code of "good" versus "bad," "right" versus "wrong." "Life is effort."	Stop putting pressure on yourself and being so critical of yourself in any way you know how immediately! Perform the Catching Negative Thoughts exercise (See the workbook). Feldenkrais will help you connect your limbs back with your core. The primary reason why RSI (Repetitive Strain Injury) occurs in the first place is that your distal extremities (hands) are working overtime without the support of the proximal musculature (shoulder, torso, and pelvis). Integration is KEY!
Respiratory (See "Lungs.")		
Rib Fracture or Strain	"let me out of here." A desire to break out free of the prison cell of your own self imposed morals and constraints.	Let go of caring so much about what others think and over-critiquing your actions and behaviors. "I give myself permission to be me!"

Ribcage (Limited Rotation and Side Bending) (See Also "Shoulder/Chest Region.")	Safety/protection: Wearing a suit of arms or straight jacket to protect yourself, protection around your heart.	Feldenkrais/yoga and other somatic practices to expand your ribcage and breath.

If you had no limitations (for instance, money, time, thoughts, other people's judgments, etc.), what would it look like to live your life fully?

(See the Rib Videos on my YouTube channel). |
| Ribs (Loose Rib or Floating Ribs) | "I'm pulling out." | Anything it would take for you to be all "in" the game of life.

(See my YouTube Rib Videos). |
| Sciatic Pain | Right leg: Exerting excess effort to walk your path.

Left leg: Stalemate on taking the next step forward. Fear or lack of clarity around the future. Or a fear of looking back at the past. | Guided meditation or Feldenkrais to assist you with releasing the muscular tension and balancing both sides of your body.

Make a list of all the places in your life you might be telling yourself: "I can't do ___ until ___ is complete." (Fill in the blanks.)

Ask yourself: "What specifically is preventing me from taking the next step forward in life; what fears are stopping me?" (List them.) "What might it take to move through such fears?"

Life Path exercise (See the workbook.) |

Scoliosis	"I'm going this way." The will of the individual is strong, if not stronger than, those whose views differ (especially with parents).	
Shin Splints, Tibial Stress Syndrome	Emotions that are numbed, nullified, and covered with hard contracted muscles or tension: This person may be experiencing a great career, financial success, a family, or life that looks ideal on the outside, yet on the inside, they are pushing through life without physical nourishment. "There's nothing wrong."	
Right Shoulder (See also Neck/Shoulder)	"I can't move forward." Or Pushing forward, responsibility, power.	For some, collaboration and working with a supportive team is helpful, for instance, having an accountability buddy. Soften your masculine, effortful, controlling, pushing tendencies.

Left Shoulder (See also Neck/Shoulder)	"I'm a marionette." Powerlessness or blocks of creativity.	Ideas to Meditate on: Step #1: See if you can "see" what the strings of the marionette represent. Step #2: Who is working the strings? Step #3: Cut the strings. Step # 4: Update your contract or subconscious agreement with yourself and this person so it feels more aligned and in the present time (See workbook). Step #5: Call back your own energy, reclaim your power and authority in your space, and do anything that will help to remove the blocks in your creativity.
Shoulder/Chest Region (Tightness Around the Pectorals Region) (See Also "Ribcage," above.)	Picture-the person locked inside a jail cell: The bars of the jail cell represents the self-imposed constraints we lock ourselves behind. Self-protection: "Boundaries" Difficulty breaking free of ideas and beliefs from the past	This protective fight-or-flight mechanism stems from the deepest parts of who we are, the reptilian layers. This is the part that when, for instance, we take an acting class and aim for unabashed expression, it falls short due to our filters and ingrained beliefs about what it means to completely let go and completely lose control. Solutions revolve around anything it might take to break free of this. Feldenkrais, yoga, breathing, anything to open up the chest/shoulder region.
Frozen Shoulder	Unwillingness to take responsibility	See "Rib," above. See my numerous Feldenkrais rib, shoulder, and breathing YouTube videos.

Sinus (See Also "Cold," If Appropriate.)	Picture-the throat area appearing tall and narrow. This constriction is due to taking on too much of what others have ingrained in you around who you are and who you "should" be, specifically around communication, decisions, walking your truth, really being heard, and blocking the toxic energies around you. Self-inflicted pressures on yourself often due to the dichotomy of being put in a "box" (for instance, regimented lifestyle) versus your internal instinct and desire to be footloose and fancy-free.	
Skin Cut (See "Cut.")		
Sleep Apnea	Worry and anxiety about the future, lack of trust in the world around you, hence, the need to be on high alert. A block at the fifth chakra: Communication Being understood	Anything that can help you flip the switch of your vigilance center off and reclaim a sense of calm and inner peace. Release control. Feldenkrais A diffuser or vaporizer with grounding essential oils can help.
Snoring	A stubbornness to change old patterns.	
Sprain (See "Ankle Sprain.")		

Swelling (See "Edema.")		
Swollen Wrists (See "Wrists.")		
Swollen Ankles (See "Ankle.")		
Swollen Joints (See "Autoimmune Disorder," "Edema," or "Finger Nodules.")		
Teeth	Difficulty taking a bite out of life. Criticism/judgment/ Indecision.	You have a right to be you! Allow yourself to enjoy the pleasures of life, for instance, really tasting your food, without guilt or self-punishment! Anything that will halt your self-criticism and monkey mind kind of thought.

TMJ (Tempo-mandibular Joint) Pain	Picture-a white picket fence that has been placed around the house. There's no gate to enter. The doors are locked shut. "Life is hard!" "You have to grin and bear it." "I want to let you in; I just can't." Self-protection	Feldenkrais: Retrain yourself to release the excess muscular tension in your jaw. One of my favorite ways to do this is by holding a wine bottle cork in your mouth for a few moments while performing daily tasks, such as cooking or cleaning. (See my book, *A Quick Guide to Easing Pain,* for more details.) Also, as explained in the neck release exercise in this book, place a hand towel rolled up under the side of your neck while lying on a firm surface on your side. Perform one-legged pelvic tilts. (See my YouTube video, *Easing Neck Pain.* This exercise is also in my book, *A Quick Guide to Easing Pain.*) Belief change work. Softening around the heart and ribs, come to a place where it feels safe to allow others in. Do heart-opening meditations and practices.
Tendonitis (Forearm)	"Life is effort." "I need to keep pushing through life."	Belief change work (See my YouTube video, *How to Change a Belief* in the workbook.) Feldenkrais to soften the excess tone/muscle effort through your fingers and arms. Retrain yourself to perform tasks such as computer work with less effort, incorporating more of the larger muscle groups. Keep all three joints of fingers slightly bent (as opposed to straight) when performing tasks such as typing on the computer, (Refer to my book, *A Quick Guide to Easing Pain*, for more detail.)

Tendonitis (Right-Thumb Extensor)	"STOP!"	Get in the habit of softening your thumb with a slight curl in it as opposed to holding it straight when performing tasks such as using the computer. Do the Putty Roll activity, which I described in my book, *A Quick Guide to Easing Pain*, to assist you in decreasing the excess tonus in your fingers and thumb. Also, there's a strong correlation with halting the breath. Hence, practice breathing regulation exercises.
Tennis Elbow/Lateral Epicondylitis (See "Elbow.")		
Elbow-Medial or Cubital Tunnel Region (See "Elbow.")		
Tetanus ("Ringing in the Ear")	"What do you want from me?" "I can't hear you." "Get off of me." Dampening your ears to prevent you from hearing the chaos around you. "I can't find my way." Confusion, obligation, a desire to come inside (thyself) and hide.	What "noise" is it that you are protecting yourself from? Is this past or present? What will it take for you to feel safe, nourished, and spacious in this world? Cutting cords (See my YouTube channel or the exercise in the workbook.) Affirmation: "The world around me is safe." Feldenkrais will help with re-sensitization and widening the perception of space inside and around you.

Thoracic Outlet Syndrome (TOS) (See Also "Nerve," "Neck Stiffness," and "Paresthesia.")	See "Nerve," "Neck Stiffness" and "Paresthesia."	Stop putting so much undue pressure on yourself. Let go of perfectionism. Take up any practice that will help you take the pressure off yourself and live in more acceptance, love, and flow. Same suggestions as for "Neck Stiffness" and "Nerve." Soften your jaw and neck. Put a cork from a wine bottle into your mouth for a few minutes when performing any basic tasks such as cooking, putting on your shoes, and typing to break the "clenching" habit. (See my book, A *Quick Guide to Easing Pain*.) Ancestral and karmic healing

Throat Congestion and Tightness	Picture-the walls of the house closing in. The house represents your place of safety and comfort and is a metaphor for your throat. The pressure from the outside world is too much. Worry and fear of what lies ahead. Feeling small and unexpressed. Blocks on self-expression and feeling heard. When this is accompanied by belly bloating, this is the perfect recipe for reflux, simply because the suppressed emotions are looking for somewhere to go. Just like if you squeeze one end of a balloon, all the air will be pushed to the other side.	Belief change and inner-child work. Anything that will help you to remove the blocks in your expression and communication—perhaps this has to do with separating your energy from another (calling your energy back), healing anger, frustration, or resentment, and finding some way to be fully expressed. Make room for you! Emotional Body and Withhold exercise (See the workbook.) See suggestions for "Anxiety," Reflux," or "Sinus." if appropriate.
Throat Phlegm (See "Phlegm.")		
Throat (Sinus) (See "Sinus.")		

Throat ('Swollen Glands")	Self-imposed roadblocks placed in the way of your desire. Holding on to the past.	Create a new reality, a new possibility of the future. See suggestions for "Throat Congestion," above.
Throat (Other, For Instance, "Pneumonia," "Thrush," Etc.)	A block in speaking your truth. "No one will hear me anyway. What I have to say doesn't really matter anyway." Feeling invisible and invalidated.	Your voice matters. Spend time around people who will listen to you and appreciate you. See other suggestions for "Throat," above.

Thyroid (Low) ("Hypothyroidism"/ "Hashimoto's")	"I've got to get this done." The urgency to accomplish things, yet something is blocking you from moving forward (frustrated creativity). Uncertainty. Pulled in many directions. Putting a lot of energy "out." A need to be on the lookout. "OH NO!" The pressure to be "on." "Next time I can do better." "Wonder woman" syndrome (do all, be all). "The world is caving in."	Belief change and inner-child work Trauma release or re-patterning work that will help you to alter your neurology, so the fight-or-flight mechanism isn't working on overdrive and you can be less reactive to life's circumstances. Feldenkrais or somatic work to soften the over-engagement of your extensor (or reactive) musculature, and to release the excess tension throughout your body. This will help you to relax your nervous system and have a truly restful night's sleep. Decrease the pressure you experience in your chest, lungs, and throat, and rather, replace it with a feeling of trust, safety, and spaciousness. Begin each morning by putting your hand on your heart and ask yourself to your heart: "What is my truth?" "What is important for me to attend to today." Organization and planning will help, as well as centering and grounding. Mantras-"I am safe." "I have spacious time to get it all done." "Everything is going to be okay." Do know that nothing is happening in your life that you are incapable of handling.
Urinary Incontinence	(See "Bladder.")	

UTI ("Urinary Tract Infections")	Picture-a tract that resembles a pistol, shooting him away from you. "Stay away." "I'm pissed off!" Suppressed anger at the opposite sex. This is most often the catalyst; then it takes eating sugar, starch, carbs, alcohol, etc., anything to have the bacteria in your gut multiply to bring this on.	There is a multitude of ways to work through anger and frustration (See the workbook). Find whichever way makes the most sense for you to get back to a place of inner peace and to reclaim your personal power. Avoid sugars, starches, and alcohol. Eat lots of healthy foods, pure cranberry juice, vegetables, etc. De-cording exercises (See the workbook or my YouTube channel.)
Uterus	Rejection of the feminine. Anger & sadness around your own childhood. Having to be the mother for others when your own mother wasn't there for you. Craving something to fill the emptiness or void in the womb (place of nourishment).	Inner Child Healing. Envision your little girl feeling her emotional pain. Then, imagine your current self holding her/loving her/embracing her. Tell her she's not alone. Commit to being there with her and loving her. Then, find a home for her to live inside of your womb. Everyday place both your hands on this area and send her love. Forgiveness practices and family healing therapies can be helpful.

Vertigo (See Also "Cerebellar Issues/Balance.") (See "Tetanus," If Accompanied by Ringing in the Ear.)	Picture-searching your way through a cloud or fog, like a blind man walking, calling for help, yet no one is responding, no one can hear you.

Energy is circulating in their head (frontal cortex) and away from their feet (or earth energy) when in this state. This results from their youngest years when trying to make sense of the chaotic, inconsistent world around them. The result of this was much dizziness, stress, and tension in the still-developing cortex of the child.

"I can't find my way." "Help me; "I'm lost." "Help me get out of here." Overwhelmed/ anxiety

The edges of their body appear to merge with the world around them, hence, making it difficult to differentiate where the boundaries of their body begin and end. Therefore, they may feel a need to pull themselves in closer to their core, as it's more comforting and safer. | The MO for a person with this experience is to stay close to home, where it's familiar and safe, despite the fact that their internal desires may conflict.

Grounding exercises (See page 179): Focus on bringing the energy from the head down to the feet.

Feldenkrais: This will help to give the person a proprioceptive sense of themselves, to know where their body parts begin and end.

Affirmations: "The world around me is safe." Pat your body, head to toe while stating, "I am here. All of me is here. The earth beneath my feet supports me."

See also suggestions for "Cerebellar Issues." |
| Virus | Powerlessness, hopelessness, feelings of invalidation. | Belief change work and anything that will expand your sense of purpose and empowerment and help you to move out of victimhood. |

Vision, Far Sightedness	Picture-fear of others coming too close. A block on seeing that which is right in front of you—fear of the present.	
Yeast Infection for a Woman (See "Infections.")	Built-up shame, irritation, and resentment. Unfulfilled energetic ties with a father or a male figure. Denying your own needs.	
Web Space (See "Hand.")		
Wrist (Swollen)	Picture yourself as a little three or four-year-old wanting to play with your Choo Choo train, and push it forward, yet fearing doing it wrong, so you halt yourself. Fears/doubts: Blocks to creative potential. "I can't, so I won't." "It's too much."	Use the train as a metaphor and ask yourself: •"What are the beliefs that are preventing me from moving the train forward? •What does the train represent? •What are my fears if I do push the train ahead? •And what might I have to give up in order to do so?" Retrograde massage, as explained under "Edema."

All of these diagnoses are holographic representations of how the individual is fighting inside his or herself from unresolved issues from the past.

Other Useful Healing Tools and Techniques

Prayer before Bed (PBB)

This is a statement/prayer I have found myself recommending more and more to clients to help them clear the energetic space around them and have a more peaceful night's sleep. I have found this also helps to create a more peaceful state of mind.

I recommend you state either of the following statements out loud while imaging the space around your body, around your bed, and around your bedroom being cleared of any unwanted energy and inviting in a peaceful spaciousness around you.

"Only the spirits, guides, and entities that are in alignment with my highest good are allowed in. All others must leave."

Or,

"Only the spirits, guides, and entities that are in alignment with my highest good are allowed in when, and ONLY when, I invite them. ALL others must leave immediately."

Grounding Technique

The term grounding refers to any technique that helps you to bring your energy down and away from your head or upper body and in the direction of the earth. Scientific research has proven how the electrical charges from the earth can have positive effects on your body. In general, grounding helps you to feel more balanced, supported, and embodied.

These are just of few ideas of techniques to ground:
- Walk barefoot on the earth.
- Hike or spend time in nature, for instance, bird watching.
- Play with your hands with clay or in a sandbox with dirt.
- Make snow angels or snowmen, if there is snow.
- Rake the leaves.
- Use your fingers to move your toes, up and down; rotate them, moving them side to side. Even just focusing on your toes helps.
- Listen to the sounds in your surroundings. Do you hear dogs barking, the sound of the refrigerator, etc.?
- Any weight-bearing activities that put pressure through your hands and feet as well as conscious movements, for instance, yoga, tai chi, and stretching.
- Pet a dog or cat or another furry pet if you have one.
- Do calm, gentle breathing techniques.
- Meditate.
- Listen to calming music and sounds like classical music and the ocean or sounds from nature, etc.
- Tend to a garden or some plants.

- Use grounding essential oils such as clary sage, cedar, frankincense, lavender, myrrh, sandalwood, and Patchouli.
- Receive or give a massage.
- Imagine a cord stemming from the base of your spine all the way down into the earth. Widen this "grounding cord," possibly to the width of both hips. This may help you to feel more supported and connected to the earth.

I Believe

We all want to love and be loved

See and be seen

Feel connection

And know our purpose

Free Unleash Your Purpose Workbook.
(See link below)

HOW TO

Unleash Your Life Purpose

And Live it Passionately!

sharaogin.com/purpose-workbook

Books, Videos, and Resources

(All written and published by Shara)

Books:

1. *Unlocking the Body's Wisdom: Accessing your Healing Power from Within Workbook.*
2. *A Quick Guide to Easing Pain in the Workplace and Beyond,* Includes written lessons, plus a free link to access six approximately 35-minute Feldenkrais audio lessons.

DVDs & CDs:

1. Chronic Pain Treatment (DVD)
2. Easing Shoulder Pain (DVD)
3. Comfort for Life – Easing Back, Arm, and Neck Pain (DVD)
4. Feldenkrais Lessons for Easing Pain in the Workplace and Beyond (CD)
5. Fitness for Life (Physio-ball exercise DVD-great for when recovering from pain)

All for purchase through Amazon or her website sharaogin.com

Free video resources:

YouTube channel (Google "YouTube, Shara Ogin").

Online Training Programs:
1. *The Body Healing Program; Awakening the Healer from Within–* 4 Feldenkrais lessons, 3 journaling exercises + more. Great for anyone in mild to chronic pain and who wants to become more embodied.
2. Intuition Development Program; Activate the 3rd Eye.

Information for both programs as well as her group programs available at sharaogin.com.

About the Author

Shara Ogin works as an Intuitive Coach, with a degree as a Reverend, a Feldenkrais Practitioner, a Life Coach, an Ergonomist, and an Occupational Therapist. She currently lives with her young daughter and husband.

Shara is passionate about helping people to remove those invisible blocks and barriers that are standing in the way of their highest potential. She enjoys leading group programs, hosting retreats, as well as working with clients, one on one.

She is the author of the book, *A Quick Guide to Easing Pain in the Workplace and Beyond,* and has produced four DVDs as well as several online programs, all focused on pain prevention and wellness.

References

Brennan, Barbara, *Hands of Light: A Guide to Healing Through the Energy Field*, Bantam, Reissue Edition, 1988.

Franklyn, Bryan. *California Leadership Institute's Coaching Training*, 12/2008–12/2010.

Lipton, Bruce. H. *"The Wisdom of Your Cells,"* June 7, 2012, https://www.brucelipton.com/resource/article/the-wisdom-your-cells.

Sheldrake, Rhupart, morphogenic fields from his various youtube videos and books.

Swan, Teal. *The Completion Process*, Hay House Inc. 2016.

Made in the USA
Middletown, DE
12 September 2022